COLLINS
BUSINESS

REVISED
+
UPDATED
EDITION

DRAWBRIDGE™

Romancing the Balance Sheet

Anil Lamba

Revised and Updated Edition

First published in India in 2016 by Collins Business
An imprint of HarperCollins *Publishers*

Copyright © **Dr Anil Lamba 2016**

P-ISBN   978-93-5029-431-4
E-ISBN   978-93-5029-432-1

2 4 6 8 10 9 7 5 3

HarperCollins *Publishers*
A-75, Sector 57, Noida, Uttar Pradesh 201301, India
1 London Bridge Street, London, SE1 9GF, United Kingdom
Hazelton Lanes, 55 Avenue Road, Suite 2900, Toronto, Ontario M5R 3L2 *and*
1995 Markham Road, Scarborough, Ontario M1B 5M8, Canada
25 Ryde Road, Pymble, Sydney, NSW 2073, Australia
195 Broadway, New York, NY 10007, USA

Trademarks
Drawbridge, Lamcon, Romancing the Balance Sheet, Figure Out the World of Figures, Finance Edge, Understanding Numbers and Financially Intelligent Organisation are trademarks owned by Dr Anil Lamba or Lamcon Finance and Management Services Private Limited.

Design by **CreativeEdge**™
www.creativeedge.net.In

Printed and bound at
Replika Press Pvt. Ltd.

Disclaimer

To Nicky, the love of my life
and Mehek & Vedant,
the apples of my eyes.

Preface

As I sit down to pen this preface to the revised and updated edition of *Romancing the Balance Sheet*, the feelings uppermost in my mind are those of gratitude and satisfaction.

I am indebted to the many hundreds of readers who have written and spoken to me... business people, executives, teachers, students, bankers and professionals, including those from the field of accounting and finance... telling me how much they have loved the book and benefited from it.

It is a source of tremendous fulfilment that, in some way, I have helped so many understand this very important subject and have been able to positively impact their business and personal lives.

I must confess to how *Romancing the Balance Sheet* got written in the first place.

I had always wanted to write a book, but could neither find the time nor muster the patience to do so. In early 2009, I happened to contract chicken pox and was grounded for about ten days. With nothing to do, I was able to retrieve this project from the back burner. In those ten days about eighty percent of the book got scripted.

While writing I used to often wonder... would anyone want to read it? This book came on the Crossword bestsellers' list the same month it hit the shelves and continues to stay there till-date, about three-and-a-half years hence.

While reading *Romancing the Balance Sheet*, quite possibly you will be able to relate the learning to your own experiences... times where you have faced situations similar to those stated, where you may have violated some of the rules prescribed in the book and suffered losses, or you may have turned around a business in trouble by focusing on the relevant ratios and principles explained, or even saved your organization from imminent collapse by diligently following the principles of good finance management.

These could even be instances where you have paid the price of carrying excess inventory, liberal credit or lax collection policies, or suffered the consequences of using short-term funds to acquire long-term assets.

I would urge you to write down your experiences, both positive and negative, and send them to me.

Maybe I can compile your experiences and create a book of case studies from which others can benefit.

In this edition I have made some revisions, modifications and additions to the matter in an attempt towards improving the content and to better communicate some of the concepts.

I hope this edition will receive an even warmer and more enthusiastic response than the first.

I have tried my best to keep the book error-free, but if any have managed to creep in, it can solely be attributed to my dogged refusal to don my newly acquired pair of reading glasses.

I look forward to your feedback.
You may write to me at **anil@lamconschool.com**.

Anil Lamba
June 2016

Contents

SECTION III
MAXIMIZING YOUR PROFITS

WHY I WROTE THIS BOOK

"I wish I had done this course thirty years ago! My life would have turned out differently."

The person who said these words to me was nearing sixty. He headed a multi-million dollar business which employed several thousand people. At this time, I was still in my twenties. I was pleased to receive the compliment and also somewhat surprised. However, as I interacted with an increasing number of people in my finance management workshops, it was a refrain I was to hear so often that it soon ceased to surprise me.

The prominent head of a large media house once confessed to me in private, "I understand the business of media, marketing and branding, but I don't understand finance".

A senior judge who had enrolled in one of my intensive finance-management programs confided that he often heard cases involving financial matters and at times felt inadequate to pass judgement.

Over the last twenty years, I have trained a large variety of people. There was one trait they all had in common, and this was a sense of inadequacy when it came to understanding figures. The inability to understand and appreciate financial statements appeared to be endemic, cutting across sectors and industries.

I was not always a trainer. Training is an activity that I wandered into without any specific plan to do so.

As a practising Chartered Accountant, providing financial consultancy, auditing, corporate law and tax-advisory services, I was often intrigued by the inadequate financial knowledge of those who run organizations.

I would find myself explaining financial concepts to professionals responsible for financial results, but who had not realized how critical these concepts were to their own successful functioning because they were not in a so-called Finance role.

The results were immediate and very gratifying. Most of them would instantly realize the importance of understanding Finance, irrespective of their area of expertise or functioning, and would appreciate what a difference this knowledge was going to make to their own effectiveness and to the organization's health. Gradually, I converted this learning into training modules, and began conducting organized seminars. These were so enjoyable to me, and so useful to the participants, that the activity grew until we, at Lamcon, were conducting training in Financial Management almost full time. Our training activities were routed through three divisions – corporate training, formal education, and distance learning.

While I once said "I also train", I now began to say "I also practice".

Today Lamcon runs a multi-country operation encompassing various facets of financial education including live training, audio and video-based products, e-learning, webinars, books, and more.

Most of our workshops are short and last from one day to one week. However one of Lamcon's programs of two-and-a-half-months duration is now in its twenty-fourth year. This program is aimed at entrepreneurs, senior professionals and CEOs of medium and large organizations. Its participant-list reads like a Who's Who of industry. A program of this duration, for people of this profile, running continuously back-to-back for over twenty years, I am told by many, could well be a world record of some kind.

This makes me feel good – but even more than that, it tells me how critically, and how urgently, the training is needed. Perhaps you are aware that of all the businesses that close down in the world, most fail due to bad financial management. It is a source of tremendous satisfaction to me that I am helping organizations and individuals to improve their financial-management skills and in the process ensuring the continued good health of their businesses.

Having observed a transformation in thousands of people, a transformation that added power and fulfillment to their careers and their lives, I wanted to share this knowledge with many more.

While I do travel to many countries to conduct my workshops, I know there will always be hundreds of thousands more who I would never have the pleasure of having in my programs. But if I were to write down all the ideas that constitute my course, they could certainly benefit from it. This is what has motivated me to write this book.

At the same time, I did not want to write yet another treatise on financial management and add to the plethora already crowding the bookshelves.

I had come to understand long ago that what the participants of my programs appreciated the most was not so much WHAT was explained (which many other similar programs doubtless also cover) as HOW it was explained.

So I decided that the book I wrote would convey the same experience to the reader as was experienced by a participant at one of my seminars. In other words, I wanted you to actually read a seminar. This is why you will find that right through this book, I have avoided jargon or textbook expressions, and am simply writing as if I am talking to you.

Before you read any further, I want you to know that this book is not supposed to be technically perfect. Finance is a common-sense subject and right through the book, I have adopted a common-sense approach to understanding it. Many of the concepts and theories to which I introduce you are my interpretations, put across in simple language, in an attempt to empower you with the ability to manage your own finances, and the finances of your organization, better.

Spreading financial education and literacy gives me immense satisfaction and pleasure. This activity keeps me extremely busy, but I find it so enjoyable that I feel as if I have never worked a day in my life. It takes me all over the world, and I am constantly meeting diverse and interesting people, from whom I learn as much as I teach them. At the end of it, when I also make money, I almost feel guilty.

CHAPTER 1

So you think you are a Non-Finance person!

Is Finance Management all about collecting and compiling financial data, recording it, and preparing the various financial statements?

Over the years, I have had in my programs a variety of participants ranging from entrepreneurs and managing directors to sales executives and housewives contemplating setting up their own businesses. Though from highly diverse backgrounds, possessing different skills and aspirations, there were two things each of them had in common.

First was the belief that they were **non-Finance** people.

Second, they all felt that finance was something complicated and beyond the scope of their understanding.

Do you think Finance Management is all about compiling financial data and preparing financial statements? If you do, you are confusing accounting with finance.

Whether it was the two-day **Eye on the Bottom Line** or our nine-week intensive **Commercial Acumen for Sustainable Growth** that they attended, by the end of the program, each one of these people left with both convictions completely shattered. They went back feeling not just thoroughly competent to scrutinise and analyse the impact of their actions on the financial health of the organisation, but also with the understanding that Finance is an integral part of their jobs and that financial principles are based on pure and simple common sense.

It is one of the primary objectives of my training to create this understanding and feeling of confidence.

As a reader, I suspect that you too consider yourself to be a non-Finance person. This could be for two reasons.

First, maybe you feel a bit daunted by numbers. Stay with me, and learn how wrong you are!
By the time you have finished this book, you will be much more in control of your key result areas, no matter what they are. The figures you deal with in your work life will cease to be a source of mystery or nuisance. Instead, you will find them comforting. You will have the confidence to make them work for you.

Second, maybe you think that finance management is about collecting and compiling financial data, reading it, and preparing the various financial statements.

If you do, it's only because you are confusing Accounting with Finance. Accounting deals with book-keeping, which is the collecting, recording and presenting of all the financial transactions of the organization. You certainly don't have to do that – that is the responsibility of the Accounts department.

Just because your job does not involve book keeping does not mean that you are a non-Finance person!
It only makes you a non-Accounting person.

In fact, there is no one who can say "I am a non-Finance person".

The ability to take financially intelligent decisions is what financial management is all about.

If Accounting is clerical, Finance is intellectual. Finance starts where Accounting ends. You may be unable to understand Accounting, but you could still understand Finance. In this book you are going to learn how to figure out the financial implications of your actions.

We are all constantly making financial decisions whether we realize it or not.

If you happen to be in Sales, and are evaluating an offer from a prospective client to buy your product at a lower rate but in higher volume, on what basis will you make your decision?
Although you will consider many factors, you must understand that what you ultimately make will not be a marketing decision but a financial one.

If you are the materials manager in a manufacturing organization, on what basis will you manage your inventory? Your efficiency is going to be judged by whether or not you can provide the necessary items on time when required by the production department. However, will it be wise for you to stock large numbers of every possible item without also considering the financial implication of doing so? Finding the optimum inventory level for each item at any given point in time is not a purchase decision but a financial one.

If you are the administration officer of a BPO and are faced with the choice of buying the next quarter's stationery at 10 percent lower than the previous quarter's price – but without the 90-days' credit you are usually offered – this is not an admin decision but a financial one. It would be irresponsible of you to make it unless you knew the financial consequences of your action.

> The ability to take financially intelligent decisions is what financial management is all about.

If you are a store manager in a retail chain, you may imagine your promotional offers to be Marketing – but unless they also bring increased profit to the organization, whether directly or indirectly, you are not doing your job properly. This means, of course, that your promotions must all make good financial sense.

Even **if you happen to be in HR in a software company**, you cannot design a compensation package, or take a decision on the bench strength, without considering the financial implication.

Whether you run your own company, lead a multinational operation, work in the ranks or are planning a start-up, you have a responsibility towards the profitability of the organization. And you will be able to fulfil this responsibility only if you learn to understand the impact of every one of your actions on the organization's bottom line.

This is the crux of financial management: the ability to understand the impact of every decision you make on the organization's profitability, and then to ensure that you take all those actions that will strengthen the bottom line and do nothing that weakens it.
This means that everyone whose actions have the power to affect the bottom line are Finance people.

Looked at in this way, the accountant is probably the only non-Finance person in the organization! The accountant is the only one whose actions do not impact the bottom line. After all the so-called non-Finance people have done their job, the accountant will compile the data, evaluate the result of their actions, and declare whether the organization has made a profit or a loss – basically just performing a post-mortem. The accountant is no doubt performing a very important job, but cannot *generate* profit for the organization.

In my opinion, it is the acts that **generate** profit that constitute financial management – not those that **calculate** profit.

Let us compare running a business to playing a game of cricket.
What is the objective of playing the game?
Simple – it is to win.
What is the objective of the game of business?
Just as simple – it is to make profit!

Now, whose actions win the game for you, is it the actions of the players on the field or the scorekeeper's?

*The Accounts person is like the scorekeeper in a cricket match.
It is not the scorekeeper who will win the match for his team
but rather the players: the bowlers, the batsmen, the captain,
and the coach who will do it.
And yet, without the scorekeeper, the match loses all its
meaning.
In much the same way, it is the actions of each individual in
every department that will help an organization succeed. If
their actions are financially intelligent, the organization will
make profits. If not,
it will suffer losses.*

So when anybody says, "I am a non-Finance person", it is equivalent to saying "I don't care what the financial outcome of my actions is going to be". But that is ridiculous. You must never do anything without understanding how it will affect the organization's profitability!

And when, in addition to your designated area of responsibility you also call yourself a Finance person, you are really saying, "I take financial responsibility for my actions".

When a large majority of the workforce says this, the organization as a whole prospers.

In any organization, there are always some people whose actions are strengthening the bottom line and others who are weakening it.

Organizations make profit when the actions of those who are impacting the bottom line positively are stronger than those who are hurting it. And if it is the other way round, it results in losses.

But can you imagine what an amazing organization it would be where everybody, as far as possible, is consciously doing only those things that have a positive impact on the profitability?

In the following chapters I am going to demystify the world of Finance for you and arm you with the ability to understand the financial implication of all your actions.

> Every person, whose actions have the power to affect the bottom line, is a Finance person.

The system of book-keeping by double entry is, perhaps, the most beautiful one in the wide domain of literature or science. Were it less common, it would be the admiration of the learned world.

Edwin T. Freedley
(1827-1904)
US Manufacturer

CHAPTER

2

The two basic Financial Statements

every Organization must prepare

All financial transactions that take place in an organization are recorded, then summarized and presented in two financial statements

All financial transactions that take place in an organization are recorded. These accounting records form the main source of information from which the two most important financial statements are prepared, the Profit & Loss Account and the Balance Sheet.

These two statements are the end result of the entire Accounting process and reflect, in a summarized form, everything that has happened over a certain period of time.

Conventionally, most financial statements are presented in a T-format. Figures are listed on either side of the T. Financial information is also often presented vertically.

In this book, we have used the conventional T-format.

You can see an example of each type at the end of this chapter.

The Profit & Loss Account

To help you understand what this financial statement is all about, let me start by asking you a few questions.

First: Why is a Profit & Loss Account made?
The answer to this question is simple and obvious.
As the name suggests, this statement is prepared to find out whether an organization has made a profit or a loss.

To go on to my second question:
Why would you want to find out whether you have made profit or not?
This question is equally simple to answer.
Let's consider three organizations: Daimler, Hilton Hotels and Microsoft. If I ask you what is the business of each of these companies, your answer would probably be:
Daimler is in the business of manufacturing and selling automobiles, Microsoft is in the field of developing software and Hilton provides hospitality services.

But the truth is that all these three are actually in one business and that is to make profit.
Their methods of doing so are different.
The primary objective of starting a business is to earn profit. Unless the business is making a profit, you might want to re-consider whether you wish to continue running it.

The third and most important question is:
How would you know whether or not a business is making profit?
Now this question is not so easy to answer.
Is it possible to wander around an organization, observe the amount of activity, check how busy the employees are, and conclude that this is a profitable business?
Can you drive through a business area, come across a wonderful-looking facility with a very impressive façade, walk inside and see thousands of industrious-looking workers and employees, each extremely occupied, and understand whether that enterprise is making profit or not?

Is it possible that the busy organization and the wonderfully-impressive facility are actually making losses?
Of course it is possible!

Is it also possible that there could be a humble-looking workshop that is making profit?
Certainly it is possible!

An organization with a grand façade, high-profile clients, an outstanding brand and impressive sales may well be bleeding dry. At the same time, a business operating from a rundown shack could just as well be highly profitable.

So what tells you whether an organization is making profit or not?
There is only one way to know this and that is if a Profit & Loss Account is prepared and studied.

It is not only a stranger driving past who cannot understand this, but even if you happen to be the owner, you would not know what the

bottom line looks like unless somebody prepares and hands over to you a financial statement called Profit & Loss Account.
The Profit & Loss Account is, therefore, made to find out whether or not an enterprise is making profit.

When we say "Profit", what exactly do we mean?

Profit is a situation where the incomes of an organization exceed its expenses. If expenses exceed incomes, it results in a loss.
In a conventional Profit & Loss Account, incomes are listed on one side and expenses on the other.

Let's look at some typical examples of expenses organizations have.

Materials consumed are expenses, salaries and wages are expenses, there are various kinds of selling expenses, money spent on rent, travelling, stationery are also expenses. If an organization borrows money to run its business, interest will also appear as an expense.

Profit & Loss Account

Expenses	Incomes
Materials	Sales
Wages & Salaries	
Selling Expenses	
Admin Expenses	
Interest	

What would appear on the Incomes' side of a Profit & Loss Account?
Income should predominantly comprise of **Sales** (of goods or services). Income appearing under the heading **Sales** reflects income generated by an organization through its core activities, that is income generated by doing the activities that it is supposed to be doing.

But organizations do sometimes receive income from sources other than **Sales**, for example, interest earned on deposits in a bank, dividends received on investments, or profit on sale of certain assets. Such incomes would be shown under a heading called **Other Income**.

You will appreciate that while the essence of running a business enterprise is to make profit, it is equally important that businesses generate profit by doing what they are supposed to be doing and not what they are not supposed to be doing.

Therefore, even if an organization is making profit, if you find that the bulk of its income comes from **Other Income**, you must still get very worried about that organization!

It is essential that income from **Sales** constitutes a major portion of the total income.

To use a bit of jargon, the sales figure, which in a conventional T-type Profit & Loss Account appears on the top right hand, is called the **TOP LINE** and the profit, which appears on the bottom left hand, is called the **BOTTOM LINE**.

Profit & Loss Account

Expenses		Incomes	
Materials		Sales	Top Line
Wages & Salaries		Other Income	
Selling Expenses			
Admin Expenses			
Interest			
Profit	Bottom Line		

Now, what is business all about? Are we in business to generate Top Lines or are we in business to generate Bottom Lines?

It is very important to always keep in mind that business is not about increasing top lines. We are not in business to generate sales. We are in business to generate profit.

But since there can't be a bottom line without a top line, generating sales is equally important.
So when I emphasize that business is about bottom line, what I mean is that we are not interested in just ANY sales. We are only interested in those sales, at those prices and credit terms, which will generate profit.

Top line is merely a means towards achieving an end, and the end is to have a healthy bottom line.

When you see the top line of a business rise and its bottom line drop, you are witnessing a tragedy. Seeing the sales figure grow could create a misplaced feeling of success unless it is also accompanied by growing profit.

The Balance Sheet

A Balance Sheet is a financial statement that lists an organization's Assets and Liabilities.

Liabilities constitute what the organization owes, that is, what it has borrowed.
When a business needs money, it borrows.
It borrows from the owners of the business, in which case it is called *Capital*.

It may sound like a contradiction in terms to 'borrow' from the 'owner'. However, for accounting purposes the owner is considered as independent and distinct from the organization.

It also borrows from outsiders, which is called a *Loan*. This is why both the owners' as well as the outsiders' contributions are reflected on the Liabilities' side of the Balance Sheet.

Other liabilities are *Current Liabilities* which include creditors, the amounts payable to suppliers and vendors, and bank overdrafts.

Top line is merely a means towards achieving an end, and the end is to have a healthy bottom line.

Assets, on the other hand, represent what it owns, or the things it has purchased by spending the money that it borrowed (as reflected on the Liabilities' side). Typical assets include investments in land, buildings, machinery, vehicles, computers, tools, etc. These appear as *Fixed Assets*.

The second category of assets, called *Current Assets*, includes items like debtors, cash and bank balances, and inventory.

Balance Sheet

Liabilities	Assets
Capital	Fixed Assets Land, Building, Plant, Machinery
Loan	
Current Liabilities Creditors, Bank Overdraft	Current Assets Debtors, Bank Balance, Inventory

To read a Balance Sheet must you also know how to make it?

An organization has a continuous stream of commercial activity with materials coming in, goods being processed, expenses incurred, sales made, equipment purchased, salaries paid, money borrowed, & so on.

It is a legal requirement that every organization should prepare a Profit & Loss Account and a Balance Sheet at least once in a year. But for a clearer understanding of the state of the business, Balance Sheets should be made and studied far more frequently, perhaps every month or even every week.

Evaluating the financial health of a business by understanding and reading its Balance Sheet is an essential skill for all the key employees of an organization.

But is it also necessary that they should know how to make these statements?

In an organization, it is the responsibility of the accountants to prepare the financial statements.
However, all who are in charge of running and managing the business, beginning with the owner, the President, and the CEO, must know how to read these statements. There cannot be a CEO alive who can afford to say, "I do not need to know how to read a Balance Sheet!" CEOs who say so are either not going to remain CEOs for long, or the organizations they lead are not going to remain in existence for long.

Sooner or later everyone realizes that their ability to lead successful businesses largely depends on their ability to read Balance Sheets.

However, a common misconception is that in order to learn how to read Balance Sheets, one must also know how to make them. This is not true at all.

It is quite possible to learn to read, interpret and understand Balance Sheets without knowing how they are made.

While everyone who is expected to read a Balance Sheet need not know how to prepare one, it's really not as difficult as many fear that it might be.

In fact, I can actually teach you how to make a Balance Sheet* in about three minutes.

Perhaps you believe that it would take much longer than three minutes to learn the art and science of book keeping and making financial statements.

> All who are in charge of running and managing the business, beginning with the owner, the President, and the CEO, must know how to read these statements.

* I have used the phrase "Balance Sheet" here to mean both Profit & Loss Account and Balance Sheet.

In fact, it takes several years, if you learn in the conventional way. But what I'm going to show you is not the accountants' method, but a far shorter way, in which we will eliminate the book keeping and directly prepare these statements using an extremely simple common-sense technique.

Let us learn how to make a Balance Sheet the layperson's way

But first let us answer a few questions:

Where does all the data that goes into the Profit & Loss Account and the Balance Sheet come from?
It is, of course, contained in the accounting records of the organization.

What exactly do accounting records record? Or in other words, how would you define accounts?
Accounts are a record of all financial transactions that take place in the organization during a particular period.

When do we call a transaction a financial transaction?
Any transaction which either brings money in or takes money out of the organization can be considered a financial transaction.

However, sometimes money may not come in or go out and this may still be a financial transaction if, at the end of the transaction, either money becomes due to you from someone else or by you to someone else.

This is to say that any transaction by which money comes in, or money goes out, or money becomes due to you, or money becomes due by you, is called a financial transaction.

And each time a financial transaction takes place, it is the accountant's job to meticulously track and record it.

A collection of such records is called accounts.

And why do organizations maintain accounts?

As we already know, the primary reason to start any business enterprise is to make profit. And profit, as seen earlier, is not so obvious.

Therefore all transactions that take place get recorded, and whatever gets recorded, periodically gets compressed.

A compressed version of accounts is presented in the form of two financial statements. One is called **Profit & Loss Account** and the other **Balance Sheet**.

> Now, this is important for you to understand, so I'm going to repeat it: All financial transactions get recorded as part of Accounts. And when Accounts are summarized the result is presented in the form of a Profit & Loss Account and a Balance Sheet.

This means that everything that happens in an organization over a certain period must eventually appear either on the face of the Profit & Loss Account or the Balance Sheet.

And between them, the Profit & Loss Account and the Balance Sheet together reveal just about four types of transactions: Expenses, Incomes, Assets and Liabilities.

This, therefore, tells you that nothing can happen in an organization which is not eventually going to be categorized as one of these four. **There are only four possibilities for any transaction that takes place in an organization.**

> So if you wish to make these financial statements the non-accountant's way all you have to do is look at every transaction that takes place, examine it, assess whether it is an expense or an income or an asset or a liability and record it accordingly. Your Profit & Loss Account and Balance Sheet will now be ready.

How does an accountant make a Balance Sheet?

The accountant looks at each transaction, takes it through a series of processes and eventually prepares a Balance Sheet.
What YOU don't understand is the process.
So, my suggestion is, examine each transaction, by-pass the process, directly record the item in the respective statement, and your Balance Sheet is ready.

Skeptical? Try this.

Imagine for a moment that your organization takes a decision to stop maintaining accounts.

Instead, it keeps a large box in the middle of the entrance lobby and each time a financial transaction takes place, instead of recording it in the books, writes it on a piece of paper and drops it into the box.

At the end of a certain period this box is given to you and you are asked to make a Profit & Loss Account and a Balance Sheet.
Can you do it?
Of course you can.
How will you go about it?

First of all, keep a template of a Profit & Loss Account and a Balance Sheet in front of you, as shown here.

Profit & Loss Account

Expenses	Incomes

Balance Sheet

Liabilities	Assets

Now put your hand in the box, take out one piece of paper at a time, look at the item listed and try and identify whether it is an income, an expense, an asset, or a liability, and record it accordingly.

Perhaps you still feel this can't be done.

Well – let's try it out!
Let's say, on the first piece of paper that you take out of the box, is written 'salaries and wages'.
Where will you record this? This appears to be an expense.

The next piece says 'travelling costs'. Also an expense. Goods or services sold? This is an income.

Any transaction by which money comes in, or money goes out, or money becomes due to you, or money becomes due by you, is called a financial transaction.

Loan taken? That's a liability.
Equipment purchased? An asset.
Interest paid on the loan? An expense, of course.
Rent and electricity payments? These are expenses.
Money invested in stocks of other companies? Assets.
Dividends received on these stocks? Income.

We can go on and on in this manner, and you will see that for every financial transaction you come up with, (or every piece of paper that you take out of the box) you will be able to classify it as either an income, an expense, an asset or a liability.

Profit & Loss Account

Expenses	Incomes
Salaries & Wages	Goods/Services Sold
Travelling	Dividends
Interest	
Rent & Electricity	

Balance Sheet

Liabilities	Assets
Loan	Equipment
	Investments in Stocks

At the end of the process you will find that the Balance Sheet you have prepared using our layperson's method is identical to the Balance Sheet prepared by your Accountant.

Do you know your Debits from your Credits?

Debit and Credit are two commonly used, yet greatly misunderstood, accounting words. I have rarely come across anybody who can confidently attribute a meaning to each of these. There is invariably a feeling that one is a gain, the other a loss; one is positive and the other negative - but it's hard to find any group of people who can reach a consensus on which is which.

The reason for this confusion is the fact that these two words, by themselves, have no meaning at all. They are used, primarily, in the context of the system of accounting in use almost all over the world, called the double-entry system of book keeping.

What is this system of book keeping?

The double-entry system of book keeping works on the premise that each financial transaction that takes place will have an impact on two account heads simultaneously.

And what is an account head?
An account head is broader than the transaction itself in scope.

For instance, if you purchase a writing pad or a pen or a box of DVDs, the relevant account head for all these would be **Stationery**. If you buy a table or a chair or a cupboard, they would come under the account head **Furniture**.

To consider an example, suppose the admin executive of an organization orders two dozen board pens. A financial transaction has taken place, and the accountant must record it in the books of accounts.

As per the double-entry system, two account heads will be simultaneously affected. In this case, which are the two account heads?

> Debit and Credit. There is invariably a feeling that one is a gain, the other a loss; one is positive and the other negative - but it's hard to find any group of people who can reach a consensus on which is which.

One is **Stationery**, and the other is the **Cash** or the **Bank** account.

The double-entry system also says that not only will one transaction have an effect on two account heads, but the effect on each of the two account heads will, as in Newton's Law, be equal and opposite.

Let's say our two dozen board pens cost 500.
Now we know that the two account heads that will be affected are stationery and cash.
Is the impact on each of these equal?
Yes, each is impacted to the extent of 500.
Is the impact opposite? Yes, because as far as stationery is concerned we have grown richer, and in our wallets or in our bank we have grown poorer.

The double-entry system of book keeping uses the words 'Debit' and 'Credit' to denote the two opposite effects of one transaction on two account heads.

One account must be debited and the other credited.

By themselves, these words represent neither good-bad, nor positive-negative. They simply represent two opposite impacts.

If you give a positive connotation to **debit** in an account, then in that account **credit** will become negative.
If you give a negative connotation to **debit** in the account, then **credit** will become positive.
Therefore a debit in a debit account serves as a plus and a debit in a credit account serves as a minus. Similarly, a credit in a credit account has a positive effect, and a credit in a debit account has a negative effect.

So, if debit and credit have no meaning by themselves, why did we discuss them?
These terms are of no consequence to a non-accounting person.
However, this will now give you a further insight into Profit & Loss Accounts and Balance Sheets.
You know that every transaction that takes place has to be, by nature, either expense or income or liability or asset.

You have now learnt that for every transaction that takes place, the accountant will assign an account head, and label it either as **debit** or **credit**. This tells us that of the four options (Expense, Income, Liability or Asset), two must be debits and two credits.

Take a look at this Profit & Loss Account and Balance Sheet, presented in the conventional T-format:

Dr	**Profit & Loss Account**	Cr
Expenses	**Incomes**	
Raw Material	Sales	
Salaries		
Stationery		
Interest		

Cr	**Balance Sheet**	Dr
Liabilities	**Assets**	
Capital	**Fixed Assets** Land, Building, Machinery, Furniture	
Reserves		
Long-Term Loans		
Current Liabilities Creditors, Bank Overdraft	**Current Assets** Bank Balance, Receivables, Inventory	

You will notice that Expenses and Assets are both debits (**Dr**), while Incomes and Liabilities both have a credit (**Cr**) label.

What further insight does this give you?

This tells you that if both Expenses and Assets are labelled as Debits,

they must be similar in some way.
On the other hand, Incomes and Liabilities must also have a similarity, since both carry the tag of Credit.

Now carefully examine the items appearing on the Expenses' side and on the Assets' side.

Do you see any similarity between *Expenses* and *Assets*?

Look at any expense, say **salary**; pick out any asset, say **furniture**.
Do you see any similarity between salary and furniture?

The similarity between the two is that in both cases money goes out.
Both involve spending.
If we spend 100,000 on payment of salaries today, it will be an Expense.
If tomorrow we spend another 100,000, but this time purchase furniture for the organization, it will appear as an Asset.

In both cases, money has been spent.
But the first time we spent the money it was an Expense;
the second time it created an Asset.

How are *Incomes* similar to *Liabilities*?

If both Expenses and Assets involve money going out, then Incomes and Liabilities must be bringing money in.

> If both Expenses and Assets involve money going out then Incomes and Liabilities must be bringing money in.

If I give you an amount of money and in exchange purchase the goods that you are selling, this receipt of money will be Income to you.

If I give you some more money, but this time as a loan, it will appear as a Liability on your Balance Sheet.
In both cases money came in, but the first time it was an Income and the second time it created a Liability.

A little while ago, I told you that it is so simple to make a Balance Sheet.

All you have to understand is that there are only four options for any transaction that takes place in an organization: Expense, Income, Liability, and Asset.

Dr	Profit & Loss Account	Cr
Expenses	**Incomes**	

Cr	Balance Sheet	Dr
Liabilities	**Assets**	

I'm now telling you that it is not just that simple.
It is twice as simple!

Broadly speaking, all financial transactions can be divided into those that bring money in and those that take money out. If money has come in, you now no longer have to choose out of four options to record it; you only have to choose between two – Income or Liability. If money goes out, choose between only two options – Expense or Asset.

How are *Expenses* different from *Assets*?

You now know the similarity between an expense and an asset. Each time money goes out, it is either an expense or an asset. But you must note that money spent is not BOTH expense and asset but either one of the two.

This means we must also know the **difference** between the two.

> Money spent on something that gets entirely consumed, before the Balance Sheet is made, is called an expense.
> Money spent on something that is not consumed at all, on the date of the Balance Sheet, is called an asset.

We must know the difference because each time money goes out, we are expected to choose – has this resulted in an expense or has it created an asset?

When is money spent called an expense, and when is it considered an asset?

The connotations **Expense** and **Asset** carry a number of misconceptions.

People often think that money spent on tangible items (like machinery, a car or a computer) are assets and on intangibles (like salary, rent, travelling) are expenses.

This is not strictly true.

Raw material and consumables are also tangibles and usually appear as expenses.

Another misconception is that expenses are small-value items like stationery while assets, such as buildings, carry a higher value.

However, large organizations spend millions on salary, which appears as an expense, while a small-value item such as a desk-top computer which may cost even less than two weeks' salary of a single employee, would be shown as an asset.

Still others are of the opinion that it is the nature of business that decides whether money spent is an expense or an asset. If **you** buy a car it will be an asset and if a **car dealer** buys a car, it will appear as an expense. Buildings purchased by real-estate traders will appear as expenses.

The truth is that none of the above criteria are relevant.

> **What really decides whether money spent is an expense or an asset is actually the life of the item being considered.**

One clue you will get is by looking at the titles of these statements. A Profit & Loss Account is always prepared for a specified period, whereas a Balance Sheet is at a point of time.

A Profit & Loss Account made annually would be titled
Profit & Loss Account for the year ending ...
If it were made monthly, the title would be
Profit & Loss Account for the month ending ... and so on.

Profit & Loss Account for the period ending...

Expenses	Incomes
Raw Material	Sales
Power	
Salaries	

The figures appearing on the Profit & Loss Account are therefore cumulative numbers for the period.

This means that if you are looking at an annual Profit & Loss Account, every figure in it represents cumulative numbers for the year.

Sales would be sales for the entire year, salary would be salary for all 12 months, and so on.

However a Balance Sheet is a statement of Assets and Liabilities as on a particular date.

Balance Sheet as on...

Liabilities	Assets
Capital	**Fixed Assets** Land, Building, Machinery
Reserves	
Long-Term Loans	
Current Liabilities Creditors, Bank Overdraft	**Current Assets** Bank Balance, Debtors, Inventory

If the Profit & Loss Account is for the year ending 31 December, then the corresponding Balance Sheet will be as on 31 December.

This means that the validity of every item on the Balance Sheet holds good only on that particular date. Not on the previous date; not even on the very next one.

For instance, if an amount of 500,000 appears under the head **Bank Balance** on the Assets' side of a Balance Sheet as on 31 December, it will mean that the organization had a bank balance of 500,000 on 31 December.

On 30 December the balance could have been some other figure and on 1 January it could still be something different.

The validity of this figure is only as on the specific date on which the Balance Sheet is made.

Financial transactions flow through an organization like water in a river. If you stop and look around you, you will see production taking place, a customer's cheque has just arrived, raw material is being unloaded, the caterer is waiting for payment, and finished goods are being shipped out.

An instant snapshot of all this financial activity gives the Balance Sheet for that particular moment.

> Money spent is not BOTH expense and asset but either one of the two.
> When is money spent called an expense, and when is it considered an asset?

Now what exactly do I mean when I say that it is the life that decides when money spent is an expense and when it is an asset?

Here are some examples which will help you to understand. Imagine that on 31 December an organization is paying salaries to its staff for the month of December, and one of its employees requests an advance payment of another six months' salary, in addition to the salary for December, and the organization agrees to pay it.

If this organization prepares a Profit & Loss Account for the year ending 31 December, and a Balance Sheet on 31 December, where will the salary for the following months appear?

It will appear on the Assets' side of the Balance Sheet. This is because the life of the salary in this case was long.

Now consider the case of a building costing millions that was purchased by an organization in October, and was destroyed by a natural disaster like an earthquake or a hurricane in November. If this organization closes its accounts on 31 December, where will the cost of the building appear?
The entire cost will be reflected on the Expenses' side of the Profit & Loss Account.

I want you to understand that a salary is not an expense just because it is salary, and a building is not an asset just because it is a building. In fact, it is the life of the item that determines whether it is an expense or an asset. When salary had a long life it appeared as an asset, and when the building had a short life, it was shown as an expense.

How long should the life be for something to be called an asset?

It might now seem that when something has a long life it should be called an asset and if it has a short life it should be called an expense, no matter what the item is, or its value, or the nature of business.

But long and short are relative terms.
How long should the life be for an item to be called an asset? How short should it be for it to be called an expense?

> What really decides whether money spent is an expense or an asset is actually the life of the item being considered.

Let me ask you two questions to bring this in perspective.
a) Suppose I buy something that lasts me for 10 months. Is it an expense or an asset?
b) I now buy something else that lasts me for 10 days. Would this be an expense or an asset?

If we only look at life in the absolute sense, we might tend to call the item that lasts for 10 days an expense and the one that lasts for 10 months an asset.

But can it be the other way around? Is it possible for the first item to be an expense *and* the second to be an asset?
Yes, it is possible.

Let's say we prepare our Balance Sheet on 31 December, and the item that lasts for 10 months is purchased on 1 January. Since the life of the item is 10 months and the Balance Sheet is prepared 12 months later, this item will appear as an expense.

Now suppose the one that lasts for 10 days has been purchased on 27 December. Life is only 10 days, but since the Balance Sheet is prepared four days later, this item will be listed as an asset.

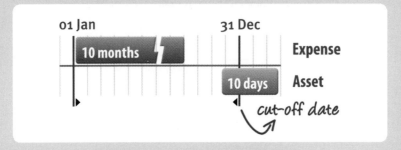

So what do I mean by Life?

Perhaps even **life** is not the best way to describe this phenomenon, since I have now shown you an item with a shorter life that appears as an asset and one with a longer life that is an expense.

Life should be seen in the context of the date on which the Balance Sheet is prepared.
Anything that outlives the Balance Sheet date is an asset.

Let me now give you the most appropriate word to understand when the money spent should be called an asset and when an expense. And that word is consumption.

Money spent on something that gets entirely consumed, before the Balance Sheet is made, is called an expense.

Money spent on something that is not consumed at all, on the date of the Balance Sheet, is called an asset.

And money spent on something that is partially consumed, and remains partially unconsumed on the date of the Balance Sheet, to the extent it is consumed is called an expense, and to the extent it is not consumed is called an asset.

A prime example of this kind of transaction is raw material.

You may have observed raw material appearing on the Expenses' side of a Profit & Loss Account, and inventory of raw material appearing on the Assets' side of the Balance Sheet as well.

Profit & Loss Account for the period ending...

Expenses	Incomes
Raw Material	

Balance Sheet as on...

Liabilities	Assets
	Inventory of Raw Material

How can the same item be an expense and an asset at the same time?

The portion of raw material that was purchased and consumed prior to the Balance Sheet date is shown as an expense.

And the portion that remained in the warehouse on the date of the Balance Sheet appears as an asset.

EXAMPLE OF A BALANCE SHEET
PRESENTED IN THE CONVENTIONAL 'T' FORMAT

BALANCE SHEET as on...

Liabilities		Assets	
SHARE CAPITAL	3,509	FIXED ASSETS	54,447
RESERVES	59,503		
LONG-TERM LOANS	45,063	INVESTMENTS	19,079
Secured 33,885			
Unsecured 11,178			
CURRENT LIABILITIES & PROVISIONS	64,471	CURRENT ASSETS	99,020
Current Liabilities 59,814		Inventory 16,820	
Provisions 4,657		Debtors 23,660	
		Bank Balances 3,123	
		Loans & Advances 52,523	
		Deferred Tax Assets 2,894	
	172,546		172,546

THE SAME BALANCE SHEET, WHEN PRESENTED VERTICALLY, WILL LOOK LIKE THIS:

BALANCE SHEET as on...

SOURCES OF FUNDS			
SHAREHOLDERS' FUNDS			
Share Capital	3,509		
Reserves and Surplus	59,503		63,012
LOAN FUNDS			
Secured	33,885		
Unsecured	11,178		45,063
			108,075
APPLICATION OF FUNDS			
FIXED ASSETS			54,447
INVESTMENTS			19,079
CURRENT ASSETS, LOANS & ADVANCES			
Inventory	16,820		
Debtors	23,660		
Bank Balances	3,123		
Loans & Advances	52,523		
Deferred Tax Assets	2,894	**99,020**	
Less: CURRENT LIABILITIES & PROVISIONS			
Current Liabilities	59,814		
Provisions	4,657	**64,471**	
NET CURRENT ASSETS			34,549
			108,075

EXAMPLE OF A PROFIT & LOSS ACCOUNT PRESENTED IN THE CONVENTIONAL 'T' FORMAT

PROFIT & LOSS ACCOUNT for the year ended...

Expenses		Incomes	
Cost of Goods Sold	47,532	Sales	72,332
Selling & Mktg Expenses	5,105	Other Income	935
General & Admin Expenses	3,003		
Interest	57		
Profit Before Tax	17,570		
	73,267		**73,267**
Provision for Taxation	2,622	Profit Before Tax	17,570
Profit After Tax	14,948		
	17,570		**17,570**
Proposed Dividend	3,518	Profit After Tax	14,948
Dividend Distribution Tax	493		
Profit Transferred to			
General Reserve	10,937		
	14,948		**14,948**

THE SAME PROFIT & LOSS ACCOUNT, WHEN PRESENTED VERTICALLY, WILL LOOK LIKE THIS:

PROFIT & LOSS ACCOUNT for the year ended...

INCOMES		
Sales	72,332	
Other Income	935	**73,267**
EXPENSES		
Cost of Goods Sold	47,532	
Selling & Marketing Expenses	5,105	
General & Administration Expenses	3,003	
Interest	57	**55,697**
PROFIT BEFORE TAXATION		**17,570**
Provision for Taxation		2,622
PROFIT AFTER TAXATION		**14,948**
Appropriations	--	
Proposed Dividend	3,518	
Tax on Distribution of Dividend	493	**4,011**
PROFIT TRANSFERRED TO GENERAL RESERVE		**10,937**

Believe nothing, no matter where you read it, or who said it, no matter if I have said it, unless it agrees with your own reason and your own common sense.

Gautama Buddha

CHAPTER

3

Do you really know what Profit is?

Does Profit mean Money?
Are we in business to make profit or
are we in business to make money?

I cannot over-emphasize the importance of profit to a business. Profit is the primary objective of running any business enterprise.

You have also understood that profit is not something that can be observed at a superficial level. The only way in which we know whether or not profits are being made is by compiling detailed information, collating it, and then presenting it in the form of a Profit & Loss Account.

Let's now take a closer look at profit.
How can we define it? How do we calculate it?

At a basic level, the general understanding is that

Profit = Income minus Expenses

(Profit, of course, could be a positive number or negative, in which case it is called 'Loss').

Let us take an example.
Let's say I start a new business and make the following transactions.

Purchase Machinery for	500,000
Purchase Raw Material for	200,000
Pay Salaries of	50,000
Sell the products made for	400,000

Can you tell from this whether I have made a profit or a loss?

I have earned 400,000 and have spent 750,000.
It may seem that I have made a loss.
But this may not be the case. You may have only received this impression because of the loose connotation in English of two accounting words Expenditure and Expense.

> Nothing should appear as an expense unless it satisfies the test of consumption.

Expense or expenditure?

Although while speaking and writing many of us use the words **expense** and **expenditure** interchangeably, in accounting they have separate meanings.

Expenditure refers to spending, or the outflow of money.

We have seen that when money is spent, we either incur an expense or we create an asset.
This makes expenditure broader in scope than expense.
Expenditure encompasses both expenses and assets.

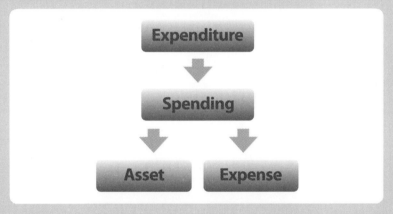

If you thought I had made a loss you probably calculated Profit as Income minus Expenditure instead of Income minus Expense!

In order to arrive at profit we must first split Expenditure into the two components of Asset and Expense, and only then apply our formula.

This is the reason why we prepare two financial statements, a Profit & Loss Account and a Balance Sheet.
Profit is not money coming in less money going out.
The money received has to be separated into Income and Liability. Money spent must be separated into Expense and Asset. And Income less Expense will give us profit.

We are now in a better position to assess whether I have made a profit or a loss.

I have spent 500,000 on Machinery. Is this an expense or an asset?
It appears to be an asset.

The money spent on Raw Material and Salaries seem to be Expenses.

The Sales figure, without doubt, has to be Income.

The Profit & Loss Account and Balance Sheet will now look like this:

Profit & Loss Account

Expenses		Incomes	
Raw Material	200,000	Sales	400,000
Salaries	50,000		
Profit	**150,000**		
	400,000		**400,000**

Balance Sheet

Liabilities		Assets	
		Machinery	500,000

With an income of 400,000 and expenses of just 250,000,
I appear to have made a substantial profit of 150,000!

In our haste to celebrate, have we made a mistake again?
We have assumed that machinery is an asset, and salary and raw
material are expenses.
However, just a little while ago we agreed that it is not the item but
the fact of consumption that determines whether money spent is an
expense or an asset.
So it is quite possible that all the conclusions we have just reached are
wrong – or perhaps they are right, entirely by fluke.

Remember: nothing should appear as an expense unless it satisfies the test of consumption.

And what is the test of consumption?
To satisfy the test of consumption, a few questions have to be asked, questions designed to create a nexus between what appears on the Expenses' side with what appears on the Incomes' side.

To illustrate what I mean, let's take another look at our transactions.

The first item on the Expenses' side is Raw Material.
The fact that raw material worth 200,000 has been purchased is of no consequence. To establish whether raw material is an expense or not, we must ask the following questions:
Was 200,000 worth of raw material purchased in order to earn the 400,000 income?
Did the entire raw material get consumed in the process of earning 400,000?
If the organization wishes to earn another 400,000, will it have to spend another 200,000 on raw material?

> **Profit is not money coming in less money going out. The money received has to be separated into Income & Liability. Money spent must be separated into Expense & Asset. And Income less Expense will give us profit.**

Only if we say "yes" to all three questions can we list Raw Material as an expense.
If not, we must ask how much was spent to earn 400,000. In case only 180,000 was consumed and the balance 20,000 is lying in the stores, then 180,000 must appear as an expense, and 20,000 will appear in the Balance Sheet as Inventory.

We must ask the same questions with regard to Salary as well. If a certain portion was paid as advance, that component will appear on the Assets' side.

The same applies to the machinery purchased.
Was machinery worth 500,000 purchased merely to earn 400,000?
If we wish to earn another 400,000, will we have to buy another machine?
If the answer is yes, the machine cannot be called an asset.

If a machine, or a building, or equipment gets consumed
– it must be listed as an expense.
If salary or stationery or raw material are not fully consumed – they must be listed, to the extent not consumed, as assets.
The ultimate test is consumption.
Let us assume that the raw material was entirely consumed and there was no component of advance in the salary paid.

Let's also assume that a study of the machine shows that it did not get consumed. In fact, the machine worth 500,000 was not purchased to earn 400,000 just once. This machine is going to help me earn similar amounts year after year, say, for the next ten years.

> Profit and Money are two entirely different things. It is certainly possible for a firm to make huge profit and have no money. It is equally possible that it is flush with funds but is suffering losses.

Now common sense tells us that if a single expenditure of 500,000 is going to help inflate the Incomes' side of ten successive Profit & Loss Accounts, then why should the Expenses' side of a single annual Profit & Loss Account be burdened with the entire amount?
That wouldn't be fair! The machine, therefore, should be shown as an asset and not an expense.

However, having listed the machine as an asset, we are still not happy. While we agree that I didn't spend the entire 500,000 to earn 400,000, it is equally wrong to say that I did not spend anything to earn 400,000.

If the expenditure of 500,000 on machinery is going to help me earn 400,000 ten times, at the end of the first year I have already earned it once. I am now going to earn it only nine more times.

This means that if not the entire 500,000, at least one-tenth of the amount should be shown as an expense.
We must therefore reduce the asset value by 50,000, and this amount will be shown as an expense in the Profit & Loss Account. This, in accounting terminology, is called **Depreciation**.

In other words, Depreciation, which appears as an expense on the Profit & Loss Account, is the consumed portion of an expenditure.

The Profit & Loss Account and Balance Sheet will now look like this:

Profit & Loss Account

Expenses		Incomes	
Raw Material	200,000	Sales	400,000
Salaries	50,000		
Depreciation	**50,000**		
Profit	**100,000**		
	400,000		**400,000**

Balance Sheet

Liabilities		Assets	
		Machinery	500,000
		(-)Depreciation	**50,000**
			450,000

**We can now see that I have made a profit of 100,000.
Profit and Money are two different things.**

Now take another close look at the transactions and financial statements that we have prepared.
Can you tell what the firm's bank balance is?
The total expenditure incurred is 750,000.
And the income is 400,000.
There is a negative bank balance of 350,000.
But I have, nevertheless, made a profit of 100,000.

Never confuse money with profit!

This is yet another common misconception.

Profit and Money are two entirely different things.

It is certainly possible for a firm to make huge profit and have no money. It is equally possible that it is flush with funds but is suffering losses.

Now if profit does not mean money, it raises an interesting question: Are we in business to make profit or are we in business to make money?

Of course, it is the objective of running a business enterprise to generate profit. But, since profit does not automatically mean money, an equal amount of attention must also be paid to the generation of cash. There is no point in making profit if, at the end of the month, there is no money to pay salaries.

Only half the battle has been won when you are able to make profit for your business. The other half will be won if you are also able to generate cash.

I will tell you more about how important this is in the next chapter.

> There is no point in making profit if, at the end of the month, there is no money to pay salaries.

The pen is mightier than the sword, but no match for the accountant.

Jonathan Glancey
Contemporary British Journalist

CHAPTER

4

How Inventory Impacts Profit

Inventory has an important role to play in determining profit.
Let's see how the impact of inventory on profit can also get misused.

Inventory has an important role to play in determining profit. In this chapter we're going to look at the various ways in which inventory impacts profit.

Imagine for a moment that I'm a trader of tables.
I buy tables at the rate of 1,000 and sell them at 1,500 each.
During the year I buy 10 tables.
By the end of the year I find that I'm unable to sell all 10.
I have managed to sell just 6 tables.
The tables purchased will appear on the Expenses' side of the Profit & Loss Account. Those sold will appear as Income.

Profit & Loss Account

Expenses		Incomes	
Purchases	10,000	Sales	9,000

In this year have I made a profit or a loss?

Although from the Profit & Loss Account as it stands now there seems to be a loss, common sense says that this should not be the case. For every table I bought at 1,000 and sold at 1,500, I have made a profit of 500. *This means that on selling 6 tables, surely my profit should amount to 3,000.*

Common sense says I have made a profit. The Profit and Loss Account, however shows a loss.

When you have a tussle between a common-sense answer and an accounting answer, which should you trust? Let me give you a word of advice. Always trust your common sense.

In this particular case, the accounts indicate a loss, but common sense tells us that I have made a profit. The error must be in the accounting.

Where is the error?

You will recall that we have established that it is consumption and not spending that is to be considered as expense. However what we have recorded here is the expenditure, or the money spent, as expense and not what has been consumed.

I did purchase 10 tables – but only 6 tables have been consumed. This means that 6,000 should have been shown as an expense and not 10,000.

The reason I have given you this example is because it arises from a practical situation that is bound to occur, time and again.

While we now agree that consumption is expense, the accountants will never record consumption. They will always show purchases as expenses.

And why don't accountants record consumption?

Because it's the accountant's job to record all purchases and sales and other financial transactions. It's not the accountant's job to track consumption.

Besides, the accountant has neither the means nor the time to do so.

In this example with only 10 tables of which 6 are sold, measuring consumption is easy. But in real life things are usually more complex.

> If you cannot track consumption for the entire period, can you at least measure non-consumption on a single day?

Large manufacturing organizations purchase enormous quantities of raw material of different types. Tracking consumption is a full-time job by itself. The accountant therefore records purchases as they happen, and shows them all on the Expenses' side of the Profit and Loss Account, without considering consumption.

But we know that if consumption is not taken into account we will not get an accurate picture of profit.

So how do we resolve this conflict?

Since tracking consumption is a difficult task, the accountant is permitted to reflect the value of purchases as expenses, instead of consumption.

The accountant is now told, "If you cannot track consumption for the entire period, can you at least measure non-consumption on a single day?"

Perhaps you know that organizations are expected to conduct the exercise of taking stock or to measure closing inventory.

In effect, stock taking is the measurement of what is not consumed.

The accountant is permitted to arrive at consumption using the next-best formula: total purchases for a period less the value of closing inventory at the end of a period, by default, will reflect consumption.

In other words, before arriving at the figure of profit, the accountant must physically ascertain what remains unconsumed on that date, and arrive at the value of the closing inventory.

In our example with 10 tables, the accountant, on visiting the warehouse to determine the closing inventory, will find 4 tables still in stock. This indicates that 6 tables have been consumed, which also means that Expense is 6,000 and not 10,000.

How is the accountant to incorporate this into the accounts?
How can the figure of 10,000 (purchases) on the Expenses' side be reduced to 6,000 (consumption)?
This could have been done very simply if it was an arithmetic problem, by subtracting 4,000 from 10,000.
However in Accounts, by and large we do not believe in plus and minus, but in debits and credits.
10,000 has been debited in the Profit & Loss Account, and if we wish to reduce it to 6,000, we must credit 4,000, and this is what we do.

The figure 4,000 will now be shown on the Incomes' side of the Profit & Loss Account as Closing Inventory.

Non-accountants tend to be puzzled at the idea that the figure of Sales (representing income from goods sold) and the figure of closing inventory (representing the value of goods not sold) should both appear as income.

Closing inventory, on the Incomes' side, does not in fact represent income, but rather a negative figure from what is shown as purchases on the Expenses' side.

Since we have shown the value of total purchases on the Expenses' side and the value of goods not consumed on the Incomes' side, the net effect represents consumption.

Profit & Loss Account - Year 1

Expenses		Incomes	
Purchases	10,000	Sales	9,000
Profit	3,000	**Closing Inventory**	**4,000**
	13,000		**13,000**

Our common-sense answer was that I have made a profit of 3,000. Now the accounting answer is also the same.

Let's now consider the situation in the following year.
I have 4 tables lying in the warehouse.
This year, I decide to purchase nothing.
I manage to sell all 4 tables at the rate of 1,500 each. What is my profit in the second year?
Have I really made a profit of 6,000? Surely not!

Profit & Loss Account - Year 2

Expenses		Incomes	
Purchases	Nil	Sales	6,000

Common sense once again comes to our rescue. My profit per table remains 500, so on a sale of 4 tables I must have made a profit of 2,000 and not 6,000.
Where have we gone wrong this time?

Though I did not purchase anything during this year, I have nevertheless consumed 4 tables.

Let me re-emphasize: it is consumption and not spending which should be considered as an expense!
So, how do we set things right?
We can do so by listing the value of goods consumed under Expenses. The closing inventory of last year will now, quite logically, appear as the opening inventory of this year.

Profit & Loss Account - Year 2

Expenses		Incomes	
Opening Inventory	**4,000**	Sales	6,000
Purchases	Nil		
Profit	2,000		
	6,000		**6,000**

Now let's look at the bank balance

What is my bank balance at the end of the first year?
In year one, I spent 10,000, and earned 9,000. My bank balance stands at a negative 1,000. However I have still made a profit of 3,000.

Let's now expand these numbers to understand their impact in a larger context.
Let's say I have spent 100 million (and not 10,000) and earned 90 million (not 9,000).
I now have a negative bank balance of 10 million.
However I have made a profit of 30 million.

Making profit can be dangerous

Do you appreciate how dangerous profit is?

Some organizations get into trouble because they don't make profit. And others get into trouble because they make profit.

What happens when an organisation shows a profit? There will be a line of people standing in a queue waiting for a share of the profit.

Who is in this queue?
First of all there are the employees, who will expect bonuses. It is they who are largely responsible for generating the profit and now expect to be rewarded.
Next will be the government demanding 30 to 40 percent (or even more) of the profit as income tax.
And of course there will be the shareholders, who will expect dividends.

In our example, I am already reeling under the impact of the negative bank balance of 10 million. But my accounts show a profit of 30 million. And the employees, the government and shareholders are all waiting to be paid. I go hoarse telling them all that I have made profits but have no money. But nobody believes me.

Some organizations get into trouble because they don't make profit. And others get into trouble because they make profit.

Successful businesses, therefore, stand on two pillars.
Pillar number one: the ability to generate profit.
Pillar number two: the ability to effectively manage cash flow.

If these two things are taken care of, most financial mismanagement-related problems will not take place.
We will go deeper into this topic in subsequent chapters when we discuss the two most important rules of good financial management.

How the impact of inventory on profit can get misused

Let's go back to my table-trading business, using larger numbers to make it more realistic.

Let's say I have purchased tables worth 10 million and not 10,000, sold tables worth 9 million and not 9,000, and I have 4 million worth of tables in the warehouse, as against 4,000.

Now imagine that I have four warehouses at different locations, and 1 million of inventory is stored in each warehouse.
A junior accountant is given the job of visiting the various warehouses to measure the closing inventory.
This junior accountant is unaware that there are four warehouses.
Somehow, he is under the impression that there are only two.

He visits the two, and concludes that the closing inventory value is 2 million. Entering these figures accordingly, he arrives at a profit of 1 million.

Profit & Loss Account

Expenses		Incomes	
Purchases	10	Sales	9
Profit	1	Closing Inventory	2
	11		11

At this point, the junior accountant's immediate senior, **who believes that there are three warehouses**, discovers that he has visited only two. He informs him about the third and the perception of inventory now changes to 3 million.

A fresh Profit & Loss Account is quickly prepared, which now reveals a profit of 2 million:

Profit & Loss Account

Expenses		Incomes	
Purchases	10	Sales	9
Profit	2	Closing Inventory	3
	12		**12**

Now the chief accountant reviews the statement.
She asks whether the closing inventory was considered for all four warehouses.
The junior accountant dashes out to complete his final visit, and his perception of inventory changes yet again, and so does the profit figure.
The Profit & Loss Account will now show a profit of 3 million:

Profit & Loss Account

Expenses		Incomes	
Purchases	10	Sales	9
Profit	3	Closing Inventory	4
	13		**13**

Now look back at these three Profit & Loss Accounts.
How does inventory impact profit?
You will notice that as the inventory figure increases, so does the figure of profit.
In the first case, when the inventory was 2 million, the profit was 1 million.
In case two, when the inventory increased to 3, the profit also increased to 2!
And, in the third case, when the inventory was the highest at 4 million, the profit was also the highest at 3 million!
This definitely seem to indicate that the higher the levels of inventory we keep, the higher our profit will be!

No business person would agree with this.
It is common sense that higher inventories do not fetch higher profits.
It is the ability to make and sell more that brings more profit.

But the three Profit & Loss Accounts tell a different story.

Where is the gap in logic?

Let's take another look at each of these cases.

Let's assume that they are actually the Profit & Loss Accounts of three different companies, A, B and C.

Profit & Loss Account of A

Expenses		Incomes	
Purchases	10	Sales	9
Profit	1	Closing Inventory	2
	11		11

Profit & Loss Account of B

Expenses		Incomes	
Purchases	10	Sales	9
Profit	2	Closing Inventory	3
	12		12

Profit & Loss Account of C

Expenses		Incomes	
Purchases	10	Sales	9
Profit	3	Closing Inventory	4
	13		13

Now A, B and C are identical companies in that each has purchased goods worth 10 and sold goods worth 9.

The only difference between the three is that A keeps an inventory of 2, B keeps an inventory of 3, and C keeps an inventory of 4.
A's profit is 1, B's profit is 2, and C's profit is 3.

Between the three, A keeps the lowest inventory and makes the least profit. C has the highest inventory and also makes the highest profit.

Again it appears that higher inventory leads to higher profit. Where is the error?

The error lies in the fact that we are making the mistake of looking at inventory in isolation. Inventory should always be seen in conjunction with purchases.
Inventory represents what was not consumed. The total of all our purchases, less what was not consumed, is equal to what was consumed.

All three companies have sales of 9.
In order to earn 9, A has consumed 8 (purchases of 10 less 2 which were not consumed).
A therefore makes a profit of 1.

B, to earn the same 9, has consumed 7.
This could be because B has more efficient people, or because there is less wastage, or because of better manufacturing processes.
B thus has a profit of 2.

C has consumed 6, taking the profit to 3.
C makes the highest profit not because it has the highest inventory, but because it has the lowest consumption.

Unscrupulous business persons, once they understand that there is a direct corelation between inventory and profit, that is, higher the inventory higher the profit and lower the inventory lower the profit, sometimes misuse this understanding to manipulate profit.

A higher closing inventory gets falsely inserted to show higher profit, or a lower inventory to show lower profit.

Royal Dutch (formerly Shell) the well-known oil company has been in the news for having shown non-existent oil reserves to the extent of 4 billion barrels to inflate profit.

Having seen in the last two chapters the various connotations of profit and what influences it, let me now turn my attention to the Balance Sheet.

> The error lies in the fact that we are making the mistake of looking at inventory in isolation. Inventory should always be seen in conjunction with purchases.

If you must play,
decide on three things
at the start :
the rules of the game,
the stakes, and
the quitting time.

Chinese Proverb

CHAPTER

5

A closer look at the Balance Sheet

How do organizations raise and deploy funds?

You have seen that the two sides of a Balance Sheet always balance.
But why does this happen?

Why can't the total of one side be more, or less, than the total of the other?

The technical answer, of course, is that Balance Sheets balance because they are prepared using the double-entry system of book keeping, in which each transaction is recorded twice, once on the debit side and then again on the credit side.
Eventually the net debits appear on the Assets' side and the net credits on the Liabilities' side.
This is why the Balance Sheet must always balance.

But this kind of answer does not appeal to the common sense.

Let's try to understand from a logical point of view why Balance Sheets balance.

Consider the Balance Sheet shown here:

Balance Sheet as on...

Liabilities (Sources)		Assets (Uses)	
Capital	30	Fixed Assets Land, Building, Machinery	75
Reserves	20		
Long-Term Loans	40		
Current Liabilities Creditors, Bank Overdraft	10	Current Assets Bank Balance, Debtors, Inventory	25
	100		**100**

As we know, the two sides of a Balance Sheet reveal Assets and Liabilities.

What are liabilities?

Liabilities represent money that the organization owes. This is money that it owes because it was borrowed by the organization.
In other words, **liabilities show sources of money**, where the organization has received its funds from.

Now what are assets?

Assets represent something that the organization possesses, something that it owns, and which has been obtained by spending the money raised.
In other words, **assets tell us where the money was spent** – the uses of money.

Looked at in this way, the Liabilities' side represents Sources and the Assets' side represents Uses.

This means that if we borrow a sum of 100 and then spend this money and purchase various assets worth 100 – naturally the Balance Sheet will balance!

What if the organization borrows 100 and does not spend all the money?
Let's say it purchases assets worth only 90.
Now how will the Balance Sheet balance?
In this case, the organization still has 10 as cash in the bank, and bank balance also appears as one of the items under Current Assets.

If an organization borrows 100 and spends 100, the Balance Sheet will balance.
If it spends less that 100, it will still balance.
Is it possible for the organization to borrow 100 and spend more than 100, say 110? It is possible.
In this case, the difference of 10 will appear under Current Liabilities as payables or creditors.
There is no situation in which a Balance Sheet won't balance, whether one spends what one has, or less, or more.

The Sources and Uses of funds

Let's first examine the sources.

How do organizations raise funds?

There is only one way:
When an organization needs money, it borrows.
It borrows from owners and from outsiders.
'Borrowing' from 'owners' might sound contradictory. However, as you know, the organization and its owners are considered as separate entities in accounting.

When an organization needs money, it has to borrow. When it borrows from the owners, it is called capital. When money is borrowed from outsiders it is called a loan. Since both are in the nature of borrowings, both appear on the Liabilities' side of the Balance Sheet.

The organization must never forget that it owes as much of an obligation to the owners as to outside lenders. When the organization is clearly aware that owners' money is also a loan, it is then more likely to treat it with the kind of diligence and respect that is usually accorded to borrowed money.

However the distinction lies in the terms of lending.

Outsiders (for example, banks) lend money on the condition that they must be paid a fixed return on their investment (interest), irrespective of whether the organization makes a profit or not. They also expect that the loan amount be repaid over a pre-agreed time-frame.

Owners impose no such condition. They neither expect a fixed return, nor do they usually expect to be repaid the principal amount of their contribution in the lifetime of the organization. If the organization earns nothing, they get nothing.

> An organization borrows from the owners and from outsiders.
> The only difference is that outsiders would demand repayment within a stipulated period, whereas owners may not expect to be repaid in the lifetime of the business.

To compensate for this risk that owners take, when organizations do make profits, the entire profits that remain, after rewarding all the other constituents, belong to the owners.

Outside lenders, who do not take higher risks, get reasonable but guaranteed returns.
The owners, who bear all the risks (of getting no rewards in bad years as well as the risk of losing their entire capital if things go wrong), get no guarantees but also have no limits imposed on the returns that can be given to them.

Let's look at this situation a little more closely, using an example to give us context.

Imagine that a new business has been set up. It needs a total capital investment of 1000, of which 400 is the owners' contribution and 600 is taken on loan from a bank, carrying a rate of interest of 10 percent per annum.

Both these items appear on the Liabilities' side as shown.

Balance Sheet

Liabilities		Assets
Capital	400	
10% Loan	600	

The money raised will be used to acquire various assets.
Let us assume that the assets, when put to use, help generate a total sales turnover of 3,000.

There will now be several claimants asking for a share of this 3,000. How many groups of such claimants can you visualize?
- One group will comprise the employees, the vendors, the landlord, the utility suppliers, the printer, the stationer, the travel agent and so on. This group represents **Operating Expenses**.
- Another group is made up of the **Shareholders** or owners who are also expecting a reward.

- Yet another group is the **Government**, which expects to collect taxes.
- And the **Lenders** also need to be rewarded.

The revenue generated by any organization will get shared among these four listed groups.

But not in the order in which we have listed them.

Let's now decide the order of payment.

The first claim on the turnover of 3,000 will be that of Operating Expenses. These get top-most priority. Come the first of the month, salaries and rent must be paid. On the due date, vendors too have to be paid. If we don't do this, we will be out of business very soon.

Let's assume the Operating Expenses work out to 1,600.
That leaves us with 1,400.
This amount is the **Operating Profit**.
This is the stage of profit at which we have recovered our Operating Expenses, but have yet to pay taxes to the government, interest to the lenders and dividends to the shareholders.
This figure is also called **PBIT** (Profit Before Interest and Tax) or **EBIT** (Earnings Before Interest and Tax).

3,000	Sales
(−) 1,600	Operating Expenses
1,400	Op Profit / PBIT / EBIT

Whose turn is it to be rewarded now?

We must now pay the lenders. As per the partial Balance Sheet shown earlier, there is a loan of 600 borrowed at the rate of 10 percent.
This means we owe 60 as interest.
PBIT of 1,400 less interest of 60, leaves us with 1,340.
This amount is the **PBT** (Profit Before Tax).
It is the amount on which we will pay tax.

Let's say that taxes amount to 340.
The resultant figure of 1,000 is now called PAT (or Profit After Tax).
PAT, as we have seen, belongs to the owners.

3,000	Sales
(−) 1,600	Operating Expenses
1,400	Op Profit / PBIT / EBIT
(−) 60	Interest
1,340	PBT
(−) 340	Tax (say)
1,000	PAT

So now, next in the queue are the owners, waiting for the 1,000 to be distributed amongst them.

The owners had agreed that if the organization earns nothing, they get nothing.

> The organization must retain sufficient cash in hand to meet its day-to-day expenses without waiting for in-flows from operations.

But when the organization does make profit, they expect the entire profit that remains, after everybody else has been paid, to be distributed amongst them. However, this will most likely not happen.

Why do you think that the PAT of 1,000, which has been implicitly promised to the owners, will not be distributed among them?
No organization distributes the entire profit amongst its shareholders.
Why does this happen?
To this question the usual answers I receive are:
"It needs money for exigencies."
"It still has to return the loan."
"It needs money for expansion."
I accept all these answers as reason number two for not distributing the entire profit among shareholders. But there is a more important reason number one.

You might recall that in the earlier part of this book, I often laid stress on the fact that profits do not represent money.

It is likely that an organization with huge profits may have no money. It is just as likely that an organization which has plenty of money may not be making profits.

Now for an organization to distribute the PAT of 1,000 amongst the shareholders, it is essential that it should first have a bank balance of 1,000, which is virtually impossible. A profit of, say, 1,000 million (i.e. 1 billion) accompanied by a bank balance of 1,000 million would be impossible. But a profit of 1,000 million accompanied by a negative bank balance of 300 million is certainly possible.

In order for an organization to pay dividends, it is not sufficient that profit has been made. It must have the requisite amount of liquid cash too.

Therefore even though, theoretically, the owners have a right to take home the entire PAT of 1,000, practical considerations will ensure that the dividend actually distributed is a much smaller figure.

Even if the organization had the money, in all likelihood the entire profit would still not be distributed amongst the owners. It would get reinvested in the business to take advantage of growth opportunities and for further expansion.
Let's say the organization decides to pay dividend at the rate of 50 percent of the capital invested *(having taken into account the cash that can be mustered and distributed without disrupting the working-capital requirement, the impact on the price of the shares in the stock market, and other relevant factors).*
The capital invested by the owners is 400.
Dividend, thus, will work out to 200.

Out of a PAT of 1,000 if dividends of 200 are paid, that leaves us with a balance of 800. Now who does this 800 belong to?
Contrary to the common misconception that it belongs to the organization, this 800 continues to belong to the owners.

By accepting 200 out of the PAT of 1,000, the owners have not waived their right over the remaining 800!
If the organization does not pay this amount to the shareholders, it continues to owe it to them.

Till yesterday the organization owed the owners 400 (the capital they had originally invested).

Today it owes the owners 1,200, the original 400, as well as an additional 800 that the organization has earned, but has not yet paid.

	3,000	Sales
(–)	1,600	Operating Expenses
	1,400	Op Profit / PBIT / EBIT
(–)	60	Interest
	1,340	PBT
(–)	340	Tax (say)
	1,000	PAT
(–)	200	Dividend
	800	Reserves & Surplus
		(Transferred to the Balance Sheet)

These retained profits will now appear on the Liabilities' side of the Balance Sheet, under the heading Reserves & Surplus.

When an organization sells goods on credit, to produce which substantial amounts have been invested, it is in effect acting like a banker to the customer to whom, instead of money, it has lent goods.

The direct contribution made by the owners (share capital) as well as their indirect contribution retained by the organization in the form of undistributed profits (reserves) together represent the **shareholders' net worth**. (Net worth also represents the difference between the book value of assets less external liabilities).

A while ago we saw that Liabilities represent Sources. And till now we have seen three principal sources of funds.

The **first**, Capital, is a direct contribution received from the owners, the shareholders.

The **second**, Reserves, is an indirect contribution, again by the owners.

They may not have physically invested this money. But they have left behind what they could have legitimately withdrawn, making it effectively an additional source. We could also say that the entire profit after tax of 1,000 was actually given to the owners, and they decided to return 800 to the organization as their additional contribution.

The **third** item is Loans. This contribution comes from outsiders.

There is yet another, a fourth, important source of funds.
Sometimes instead of borrowing money, organizations borrow goods.
When goods are purchased from vendors on credit, it amounts to a loan, not in cash but in kind. These appear on the Liabilities' side as creditors.

This is how the Sources' side of the Balance Sheet will now look:

Balance Sheet

Sources		Uses
Capital	400	
Reserves	**800**	
= Net Worth	**1,200**	
10% Loan	600	
Creditors	200	

Should you have less money or more?

One important question we must consider here is, why is this organization going around collecting funds from all and sundry?
It collects money from the owners, and also from outsiders.
It collects from owners directly as well as indirectly.
From outsiders it takes loans in cash and also in kind.
Is this an arbitrary collection of money or must it be as per a plan?

The answer is that if this organization wishes to be successful, its collection of funds had **better** be as per a plan!

What will happen if there has been an unplanned garnering of resources?
If the resources have been raised without a definite plan in mind, when this organization starts investing, it will discover that it either has less money than it requires or more; that is, either it will run short of money mid-way in the process of acquiring assets, or it would have purchased all the assets it needs and still have money left over.

Which do you think is a happier situation?
Should you have less money or more?

It is quite obvious that if an organization has less than the required funds available, it will suffer from the consequences of shortage. It is sure to get into trouble.
However, if an organization has more money than it needs, it is going to get into even bigger trouble.

Now everybody understands the problems that can arise if one is short of funds.
What is less easy to understand is how one can get into trouble if one has more!
This I will explain in the next chapter.
But you must always remember the mantra for success in business, and that is: Less is bad; more is worse!

Should you maintain higher inventory or lower?
Should you have a larger amount in the form of receivables and debtors or a smaller?
Should you have more of a bank balance or less?

There's a simple answer to these questions, and it is: **neither**. All these should be at an optimum level.
Remember: less is bad; more is worse.

Let's now look at the
Uses' side of the Balance Sheet

Where will a typical organization spend the funds it collects?
A substantial portion of the funds collected will be invested in the creation of infrastructure.
Every organization needs to invest in various kinds of assets required to run its business.
A manufacturing company will need to invest in land, building and equipment.
A trader needs to invest in showrooms, warehouses and offices.
A software company will invest in equipment, licenses and furniture.

Such investments appear in the Balance Sheet under the head **Fixed Assets.**

Even if a substantial portion of the total resources goes into infrastructure, businesses must ensure that all the funds do not get exhausted in the creation of infrastructure alone.

There should be money left after purchasing fixed assets, since to put the infrastructure to use a business needs a continuous supply of **Working Capital.**

What are the components
of working capital?

Let's take the case of a manufacturing organization. It invests a large amount in purchasing excellent infrastructure, but exhausts all its resources in the process.

It now receives a large order. Do you think the organization will be able to execute the order? Probably not.

A few rare and extremely fortunate organizations are able to command the entire invoice value, or even a portion of it, as advance payment from the customer.

The mantra for success in business is: Less is bad; more is worse!

In most cases, this will not happen. They now need to buy the raw material for the order. In fact, prudent businesses do not procure raw material after the order is received, but will buy and keep an inventory of raw material, so that production can commence immediately on receipt of an order.

The first and foremost requirement of working capital, therefore, is in order to acquire and maintain inventories.

The large order that the manufacturing organization received needs about three months time to be executed.

However, the first of the month is round the corner! The employees are expecting salaries, the landlord is expecting rent, and all the other overheads also have to be paid. Employees and others cannot be told that they will be paid only after the money is received from customers after delivery of the goods ordered. *Organizations must understand that incomes are sporadic while expenses are continuous.*

This means that the organization must retain sufficient cash in hand to meet its day-to-day expenses without waiting for in-flows from operations.

Thus, adequate cash and bank balance is yet another component of working capital.

Finally, after three months of hard work, the organization completes the order. The client approves the consignment and requests that delivery be made. But the terms of sale were that payment would be made 60 days after delivery!

Having invested a substantial amount in this order, the organization must now possess the ability to sustain itself financially for another two months, during which time the routine work and all expenses related to it will continue.

Debtors now become the third component of working capital.

When an organization sells goods on credit, to produce which substantial amounts have been invested, it is in effect acting like a banker to the customer to whom, instead of money, it has lent goods.

Balance Sheet

Sources		Uses	
Capital	400	**Fixed Assets**	**1,500**
Reserves	800		
= Net Worth	**1,200**		
10% Loan	**600**		
Creditors	**200**	**Working Capital** Inventory, Debtors, Bank Balance	**500**
	2,000		**2,000**

To sum up

In a Balance Sheet, Liabilities represent Sources, and Assets represent Uses of funds.

There are two principal sources of funds, Owners and Outsiders.

Each invests in two ways.
Owners make a direct contribution when they invest their money, and an indirect contribution when they leave behind the profits which they were entitled to take home.

Outsiders invest by either lending money (loans) or by lending goods (suppliers' credit).

The resources so raised are deployed in two ways:
towards creation of infrastructure (purchase of fixed assets) and towards working capital.
Working capital has three components, namely inventory, cash and bank balances, and debtors or receivables.

With this, you are now ready to move on to the next chapter and receive one of the most important lessons that I am going give you in this book and that is, how to practice Good Financial Management at all times.

The surest way to ruin a man who does not know how to handle money is to give him some.

George Bernard Shaw
(1856-1950)
Irish Critic and Playwright

CHAPTER

6

Good Financial Management
The Two Golden Rules

If these two rules are diligently followed, most problems caused by financial mismanagement can be avoided

What is it that causes businesses to fail?

Contrary to popular perception, most businesses that fail have not done so on account of inferior quality of products, or marketing inefficiency, or even labor problems. In fact, **the single largest cause of business failure the world over is financial mismanagement**.

This happens due to a widely-held belief that managing Finance is the job of the Finance Department alone. As you now know, much of what happens in the Finance Department is largely accounting-related. Financial management, on the other hand, is the job of every individual in the organization.

I am not trying to suggest that good financial management alone can make organizations successful. Without a good product and effective marketing skills, without a committed and capable team, you are unlikely to enjoy great success.

> **Good financial management, by itself, cannot lead to success, but bad financial management can single-handedly spell doom for any business.**

I cannot adequately stress the damage and grief that can be caused by financial mismanagement. Everybody across the organization must have financial management skills. Every single member of every team in the organization must learn, understand and practise good financial management.

So what exactly is Good Financial Management?

The answer to this question can be very long and include every principle of financial management.
But for that you will have to enroll in a professional finance program.
Let me give you, instead, a short and succinct formula in the form of two rules for what, in my opinion, comprises good financial management.
Let's call them the two golden rules of good financial management.

Read these rules carefully. Read as if your life depends on them!

> **Financial management is merely the ability, on the part of EVERY individual... to understand the financial implication of EVERY action.**

If you ensure that you never violate either of these rules, I promise you that you will never face most of the problems others do on account of bad financial management.

To appreciate the relevance and depth of these rules, you must think like an entrepreneur. So, before you read any further, put on your entrepreneur hat! If you are an employee in an organization, you must be an entrepreneurial employee. If you are an owner – encourage and empower your employees to think like owners. Remember – the best decisions are made when everyone thinks and behaves like an owner.

The first rule of Good Financial Management:

> **Never invest your money without ensuring that the assets you acquire can generate a return which is at least equal to the cost of your capital.**

Let me explain what I mean by this.

To apply and understand the two golden rules of good financial management, you will need to refer to a Balance Sheet.

You already know that the Liabilities' side of a Balance Sheet represents sources of money, and the Assets' side represents uses of money.

The sources from which organizations borrow are many.
What you must remember is that of all the sources, none are free.
The money that an organization raises comes at a cost. Very often we lose sight of this cost, and then pay a price that is far too high. Don't forget, there are no free lunches in this world!

And what do organizations do with the resources they raise?

They deploy them to purchase assets. These assets are, presumably, productive assets with an ability to earn.

The first golden rule urges you to invest only after ensuring that the returns you can generate are either equal to, or preferably greater than, the corresponding cost of sources.

> The best decisions are made when everyone thinks and behaves like an owner.

What does the application of Rule I imply? It implies knowledge on your part about your **cost of capital** and an ability to project the **returns that can be generated** through the deployment of your funds.

Invest only after ensuring that the projected returns are either equal to, or greater than, the cost.

If I ask you to lend me some money and offer to pay you 10 percent interest, should you say "yes" or "no" to this investment opportunity?

The answer depends on your cost of capital.

You need to know how much the money you are contemplating lending is costing you.

If it costs you less than 10 percent you can say "yes".

But if it costs more than 10 percent you must say "no".

Before I elaborate further on Rule I, let me tell you what the second rule is.

The second rule of Good Financial Management:

Invest your money in such a way that the assets will generate an inflow of funds before the liabilities demand an outflow.

You must recognize that in a business organization, **all sources of funds are liabilities and not gifts**. The money you have raised today will have to be repaid tomorrow.

When I requested a loan from you, even if the opportunity satisfies Rule I (that is, your money costs you less than the return I am offering) you may still refuse if you find that Rule II is being violated.

What if you have borrowed this money from a source that wants it back in the next 30 days and I can return it to you only after 60 days? This investment opportunity is now violating Rule II as per which you must only invest after ensuring that the asset can generate an inflow before the liability demands an outflow.

While these are just common-sense rules, you will be surprised how many large organizations run by competent professionals are guilty of violating them.

Although I don't need to tell you that you can't borrow money at 10 percent and then lend it at 5 percent, I would urge you to understand that the interpretation of what the money is costing you is critical, and it is subjective, and this is where you must be careful.
Being aware of the cost of your capital will also make you more sensitive to the viability of every new business opportunity, and every financial decision that you need to make.

> Invest only after ensuring that the asset can generate an inflow before the liability demands an outflow.

Similarly, being constantly aware of the need to be able to return the money when it becomes due will make you alert to putting it to the best possible use in the time given to you to use it.

Businesses looking for long-term and genuine success must never let these two principles out of their minds.

In the next chapter I will elaborate on the first Rule and in the following chapter I will explain Rule II in greater detail.

Yesterday is a cancelled cheque. Today is cash on the line. Tomorrow is a promissory note.

Hank Stram
US Football Coach

CHAPTER

7

Improving Profitability

Applying lessons from Rule I

Know your Cost of Capital,
Keep Non Performing Assets in check,
Sweat your Performing Assets

Let us now discuss the first rule at length.

Rule I of Good Financial Management

As per the first rule, you must never invest your money in any opportunity where you cannot generate a return which is at least equal to your cost of capital.

The prerequisite to ensure that Rule I is not violated is knowledge about cost of capital.

Every businessperson, entrepreneur, and key employee must be constantly aware of the cost of capital applicable to the organization so that everybody can then, collectively, strive to generate a return that justifies the cost.

My experience, however, is that many are absolutely ignorant about their cost of capital. They are constantly engaged in trying to generate income.

Now stop and think about this for a minute. Unless you know what your cost of capital is, how can you possibly know whether the returns you are so busy generating are sufficient or not?
Unless you can earn in excess of your cost, all your activity and effort will be futile.
You would never lend your money on a return of 10 percent when your funds cost you more than 10 percent … **provided you know what your funds are costing you.**

The truth is that most people are unaware of the cost of their capital.

I have interacted with many thousands of highly placed and highly successful individuals.
When I ask a group of assembled entrepreneurs in a training session, "How many of you know your cost of capital?
Do you know how much your funds are costing you?"
very few hands go up. I find this lack of knowledge about cost of funds very alarming.

Perhaps you don't believe that the situation is quite as bad. Well, in that case let me put the same question to you. Are you aware of your cost of capital?

If you are an entrepreneur or a CEO, and if you cannot answer this question immediately, if you start humming and hawing, there is cause for concern.

Let us now understand how cost of capital can be calculated.

Take a look at this Balance Sheet:

Balance Sheet

Liabilities		Assets	
Capital	300	Fixed Assets	750
Reserves	200	Current Assets	250
12% Loan	400		
Creditors	100		
	1,000		**1,000**

Looking at this Balance Sheet, can you tell how much its capital is costing this business?
But first, before you work out the cost of capital, try to see if you can assess how much the capital itself is.

In case you are not able to do so immediately, please don't worry. When we do this exercise in my workshops, I invariably get a range of different answers made up of various combinations of the numbers that appear on the Liabilities' side of the Balance Sheet.

In this Balance Sheet, and for the limited purposes of this discussion, 1,000 must be considered as the capital.
What is the logic of Rule I? Rule I tells us that we must understand what the left hand side of the balance sheet costs us and then strive to ensure that the right hand side earns as much as, or more than, that amount.

We must, therefore, ascertain the cost of the entire Sources' side.

But the 1,000 on the left hand side is composed of four items:
1) **Capital**
2) **Reserves**
3) **Loans** carrying interest at a rate of 12 percent
4) **Creditors**

Before you read any further, stop for a minute to look back at the Balance Sheet and examine each of these figures and ask yourself which of these sources costs the organization.

The first figure, **capital**, is the owners' contribution. Owners, as opposed to lenders, are not assured any returns. Owners are risk-bearers. If the organization makes losses, the owners do not get anything. However, since they carry the risk of not getting returns and even losing their money, their reward is that there are no limits to how much they can earn, subject to availability of profits. However there is no compulsion on the organization to reward the owners. *Therefore, it is often perceived that owners' money is free.*

Now what about **reserves**?
Reserves represent profits retained within the business.
Even when an organization declares dividends, it is only a percentage of the share capital. No dividend is paid on reserves. *So can we assume that reserves are available for the organization to use free of charge?*

The next item is **loans**. Everybody understands that loans have a cost. There is a stated commitment to pay a stipulated rate.

The lender has also made it clear, at the time of lending the money, that the promised return will be due regardless of whether the organization makes a profit or a loss. And to ensure compliance, assets worth far more than the value of the loan have been assigned to the lender as security. In addition, if the lender is not paid, the organization will lose credibility and its future borrowing capability may be jeopardized.

> Owners' money is far more expensive than borrowed funds.

It's clear that loan funds definitely carry a cost. *Calculated at 12 percent in this case, it works out to 48.*

What about the last one, the **creditors**?
This figure often represents the amount due to vendors for goods purchased on credit. If you make a purchase worth, say, 100, payable after a month, the vendor expects to be paid the same 100, without any addition of interest on that amount.
This makes creditors a free source of money.

In this Balance Sheet, only loans of 400 have been taken at a cost of 12 percent, which works out to 48. The total sources are 1,000 and the cost is 48. So it appears that the average cost of capital is 4.8 percent.

Anyone with a perception that the cost of capital is 4.8 percent might refuse an investment opportunity that brings a return of, say, 4 percent, and grab another with the potential to earn 6 or 8 or 10 percent, and feel satisfied that they are taking sound investment decisions.

However, this perception of cost of capital is flawed, and can invite serious trouble!

Let's take a closer look at all the sources of capital and understand which of them has a cost.

1) Capital: Does owners' capital have a cost?
Stop for a minute and think. Why would anyone want to start a business?
Businesses are started with the primary objective of making profits for the owner.
If the lender has invested with the objective of earning money – so has the owner!
And if the lender expects to earn 12 percent with all the assurances and security of assets to fall back on in case things don't work out, doesn't the owner, for whose benefit the business is really being run, and who carries all the risks of losses, deserve a substantially higher return?

The return that owners would expect will vary from situation to situation, and person to person, but, in my opinion, taking even the most pessimistic approach, it should be at least twice what the lender is charging.

In this example loans cost 12 percent. **So let us consider the cost of owners' money to be 24 percent.**

2) Reserves: What about Reserves?
Reserves represent undistributed profits which have been ploughed back into the business.

If a Balance Sheet has reserves as one of the items on the Liabilities' side it means that the shareholders of the organization have been deprived of dividends to that extent.

Who is it that has deprived the shareholder of dividends? Who has taken the decision to distribute the profits among owners or retain them in the business?

In a proprietary concern this would be the proprietor, in a partnership firm it is the partners, and in a joint stock company, it is the shareholders (via their elected representatives, the directors).

Now the question to be answered is:
How can the directors, who were elected by the shareholders to protect their interests, take a decision that goes against the interests of the shareholders?
On what basis can the board tell its shareholders, "We have made profits, but we are not going to give them to you?"

It can only be done when the decision to give dividends to shareholders is in the interest of the shareholders, and a decision not to give them dividends is also in their interest. And the only way in which a decision not to give money to the shareholders can be in their interest is when the board of directors carries the conviction that, given the reinvestment opportunities available with the company, it is possible to earn higher returns for the shareholders by keeping the money within the company than it is for the shareholders to earn for themselves by taking the money out of the company.

What I am trying to get at is that whenever an organization transfers profits to reserves, thereby depriving shareholders of dividends, it has also deprived them of the opportunity to earn on that amount by reinvesting the dividends.

The corporation is under a moral obligation to generate a return on the retained profits which is at least equal to the opportunity denied.

Let us consider the opportunity cost of Reserves to be 15 percent (even though there is a strong case to attribute the same cost to reserves as to share capital).

3) Loans: **In this case, loans carry a committed cost of 12 percent.**

4) Creditors: It is true that vendors do not charge interest when they are paid on the due date. However, as most businesspeople will vouch, any creditor will readily offer a cash discount ranging from one to two percent per month (and sometimes more) for payment received before the specified time. One to two percent discount per month works out to 12 to 24 percent per annum. The creditor can afford to give this discount, because this interest had already been factored into the quotation given by the vendor for supply of goods on credit.

For the purpose of the Balance Sheet we are discussing, **let's assume an average cost of 18 percent per annum.**

And now let's take another look at our Balance Sheet and calculate the weighted average cost of capital.

Balance Sheet

Liabilities		Assets	
24% Capital	300	Fixed Assets	750
15% Reserves	200		
12% Loan	400	Current Assets	250
18% Creditors	100		
	1,000		1,000

Calculation of
Weighted Average Cost of Capital (WACC)

300 from the SHAREHOLDERS @**24**% ➡ 72

200 by way of RESERVES @**15**% ➡ 30

400 from BANK LOANS @**12**% ➡ 48

100 from CREDITORS @**18**% ➡ 18

TOTAL CAPITAL is **1000**   COST is **168**   WACC is **16.8**%

The Weighted Average Cost of Capital is actually 16.8 percent, and not 4.8 percent as we had previously assumed.

If sources cost this organization 16.8 percent, then any investment in assets is justified only if a return of not less than 16.8 percent per annum, or profits not less than 168 on an investment in assets worth 1,000, can be generated.

Many entrepreneurs I meet are either ignorant of their cost of capital, or carry the impression that only loan funds carry a cost, and thus arrive at a number similar to the 4.8 percent we earlier calculated.

And when they get into financial trouble by taking on projects earning less than the actual cost of capital, they simply cannot figure out what went wrong.

> **It is very important to remember that no source of capital is free, least of all the owners' contribution. Owners' contribution is not only not free, but it is actually the most expensive source of money.**

It's not only outsiders who make this assumption but very often owners themselves think that their money is free!

I have known owners, who, while evaluating a project, look at income projections and exclaim, "This project can't afford borrowed resources. Let us use our own funds!"
If a project cannot afford borrowed money, it definitely does not deserve owners' money. Never forget that owners' money is far more expensive than borrowed funds.

As you may have noticed, I have been saying "Investment in assets must generate a return **equal to**, and preferably greater than, the cost of capital".

Financial management is the collective responsibility of the ENTIRE organization.

Why "**equal to**"?
Shouldn't I be saying, "Assets must always generate a return **greater than** the cost of capital"?
Let me explain.
What happens when the returns are equal to the cost of capital?
In the Balance Sheet we are scrutinizing, we have calculated a cost of 16.8 percent. We arrived at this figure taking into account everybody's expectation of returns, including a 24 percent return for the owners.

When the organization generates a return equal to the cost, that is a return of 168 on an investment in total assets of 1,000, all those who have provided resources earn what they are expecting to earn.

But what happens when the returns are somewhat lower than the weighted average cost of capital (WACC)?

All the other stakeholders of the business, the employees, the vendors, the lenders – will be paid.

The only one who will receive less than expectations is the owner. How ironical!

The business was started with the primary motive of making profits for the owner – and the owner is the only one who is not getting the desired returns.

And what if the business earns in excess of the WACC?

The employees, the lenders, the vendors will still get the same amount. But the owners will get a return higher than 24 percent.

To have out-performed the owners' expectations is to have truly succeeded.

When will Rule I be satisfied?

In the Balance Sheet we have been discussing, the WACC is 16.8 percent.

To satisfy Rule I, the organization must ensure that the investment in assets generates a minimum return of 16.8 percent. The investment of 1,000 in assets will be justified only if the returns are a minimum of 168.

But hold on for a minute.

Do all assets generate income? No, they do not.

If you make a list of all the assets a business typically possesses (land, buildings, equipment, vehicles, furniture, stocks of raw material, fittings and fixtures, and so on) you will find that **it is possible to classify all assets into two types: Performing Assets (PAs) and Non-Performing Assets (NPAs).**

Every organization is bound to possess assets which can be called NPAs.

By non-performing, I do not necessarily mean non-essential assets or those that are not required.

Non-Performing Assets are those assets that do not directly generate income for the organization.

> Whenever there are Non-Performing Assets in an organization, the expectation from the Performing Assets becomes that much higher.

The furniture in your office, for instance, is essential but does not generate income.

Your car is a Non-Performing Asset, but a taxi-driver's car is a Performing Asset.

Some assets earn for the organization, while others do not.

Let us assume a break-up between PAs and NPAs of 50:50. There will be organizations with a better PA vs NPA ratio, while there will be others with a worse ratio.

Now how does this change the equation?

Going back to our example, the minimum return we required to generate was 168 on an investment of 1,000. However, since 50 percent of the assets are NPA, it is only the remaining 500 worth of assets that are expected to generate 168. **This now takes our targeted rate of return to 33.6 percent.**

Hold it once again. Think for a minute. **Do Performing Assets perform throughout the year?**

Many organizations follow a five-day week. In addition, if we count national holidays and festivals and take leave entitlements and maintenance shut-downs and breakdowns into account, it has been estimated that even Performing Assets effectively perform for two-thirds of the year.

But do you realize that liabilities perform throughout the year! No banker offers not to charge interest for the weekend!

So considering that our assets are supposed to generate a return of 33.6 percent, which has to be achieved over two-thirds of the year (since for the remaining one-third they are not performing), **the effective targeted annualized rate of return now goes up to 50.4 percent.**

Calculation of the Real Cost of Capital

TOTAL CAPITAL is **1000**   COST is **168**   WACC is **16.8%**

PA	NPA	➡ **33.6%**
50%	50%	

If PAs perform for 2/3rds of the year   ➡ **50.4%**

If you are an entrepreneur or a business owner who is reading this and realizing these truths for the first time, I'm sure you will not sleep tonight!

This organization will now have to earn at the rate of 50 percent plus in order to meet every stakeholder's expectations.

What I am trying to do through detailing and dissecting matters in this way is to drive home the message that **every organization must realize it does not possess any asset**, no piece of equipment or motor car or laptop **which does not have a corresponding liability. And there is no liability which does not have a cost.**

To quickly grasp the relationship between PAs and NPAs, let's take the analogy of a household with a family of 10 members and a monthly expenditure of 1,000.
If each member were to work and contribute an amount of 100 towards monthly expenses, the distribution would be fair. However, in a family of 10, if 5 members are NPAs (since they may be too young or too old to work and earn) and only 5 are PAs, each PA will have to contribute 200.

Whenever there are NPAs, the expectation from the PAs becomes that much higher.
The higher the NPAs, the bigger the burden on the PAs to perform for themselves as well as for those who do not perform.

Perhaps you will now see more sense in my mantra "Less is bad, more is worse". Less results in shortages, and more is NPA.

> **Cash-in-hand beyond what is necessary is a non-performing asset.**

If all your assets are Performing Assets, and if the cost of your sources is, say 10 percent, your assets must generate a return of 10 percent.

However, if half your assets are NPAs, the PAs must earn at 20 percent.

If the PAs perform for two-thirds of the year, they must generate a return of 30 percent.

All this is going to make you run faster and faster just to stay in the same place.

> **Perhaps you will now see more sense in my mantra "Less is bad, more is worse". Less results in shortages, and more is NPA.**

Holding inventory is necessary for a manufacturing organization – but inventory in excess of what is required is a non-performing asset. It may be the norm to extend credit to customers – but if the salesperson offers customers 45 days credit, when with a little negotiation he or she could have managed to sell on 30 days credit, the excess of 15 days is non-performing.

Cash-in-hand beyond what is necessary is a non-performing asset. **Every investment in excess of the optimum level is non-performing. Never forget – less is bad, more is worse!**

If the Liabilities or Sources of Funds are composed of a higher proportion of cheap money and a lower proportion of expensive money, and if the Uses side has a higher proportion of PAs as compared to NPAs, the profitability of organizations in such cases will be the highest.

In the next chapter, let us discuss and understand Rule II of Good Financial Management, and also learn how to read a Balance Sheet using that understanding.

It sounds extraordinary, but it's a fact that balance sheets can make fascinating reading.

Mary, Lady Archer
(1944-)
British Chemist

CHAPTER

8

How to Read a Balance Sheet

using the Rule II Perspective

A good Balance Sheet for an equity investor may not be so for a lender.
What is the best way to describe a healthy organization?

**Let us now turn our attention to the second rule.
As per this rule you must invest your money in such a way
that the assets will generate an inflow of funds before the
liabilities demand an outflow.**

In the process of studying Rule II, you will also learn how to read a
Balance Sheet.
In fact, I believe that to a certain extent you already know how to do
this.
In case you disagree, let me prove it to you.

Let's imagine that you are a banker and two individuals, A and B,
approach you for a loan.
You ask both to bring you their Balance Sheets.

Take a look at their two Balance Sheets, reproduced here.

Balance Sheet A

Liabilities		Assets	
Share Capital	450	Fixed Assets	750
Reserves & Surplus	300		
Long-Term Loans	200	Current Assets	250
Creditors	50		
	1,000		**1,000**

Balance Sheet B

Liabilities		Assets	
Share Capital	150	Fixed Assets	750
Reserves & Surplus	100		
Long-Term Loans	650	Current Assets	250
Creditors	100		
	1,000		**1,000**

Study the two Balance Sheets carefully. If YOU were the lender who would you be inclined to favor?

Which one of these would you feel comfortable lending to and which one would you be reluctant to give a loan to?

If you have reached ANY conclusion based on your study of the two financial statements, you have just read a Balance Sheet.

If you voted in favor of A, I would agree with you.

Let's now discuss what it is about A that gives confidence to the lender.

Both A and B seem to be similar as far as the Assets' side is concerned. The difference is on the left hand side of the Balance Sheets. It lies in their method of funding.

The first thing to remember about analyzing a Balance Sheet is that perspectives vary. What is a good Balance Sheet for an equity investor may not be so for a lender.

In this case, you were asked to wear the hat of a banker, a lender.

Now how is a banker as an investor different from an owner who also invests?

The difference is that an owner not only invests the money but is also responsible for running the business.

A lender, to that extent, is a passive investor, making only a financial investment and having no other involvement. Thereafter, whether the investment will be serviced on time and whether the loan will be repaid on time or not depends on how well the owner, who is the active investor, runs the business.
If the owner is totally involved in the running of the business, gives it enough time and attention, and is able to bring good results, the lender's investment will be protected.

However if the owner messes up by neglecting the business or managing it badly, the lender will also suffer.

An owner whose personal investment in the business is substantial is likely to be more committed to its success, and more involved in its running.
However, if the owners' financial stake in the business is small, and consequently stands to lose less if the business runs into trouble, the lender is justified in fearing the possibility of neglect. Perhaps the owner has larger investments in other businesses, and would devote more time and effort to those.

A lender, consequently, derives comfort from a situation where the owners' stakes are higher.

In the case of Balance Sheet A, out of a total asset base of 1,000, the owners' contribution, direct plus indirect, is to the extent of 75 percent. In the case of B the direct contribution of the owner is merely 15 percent, and including reserves, it works out to 25 percent. The bulk of the funding has come from outsiders. If B gets into trouble, the outsiders stand to lose far more than the owners.

A lender must also take into account the **worst case scenario** before making a decision.
What is the worst thing that can happen once you have lent the money? The business may fail.
If this happens, the only way to recover the money would be by selling the company's assets.

The total of the Assets' side in both cases is 1,000. However, when a business closes and there is a distress sale, assets often fetch a value that is far lower than their book value.
It's also possible that some assets which appear on the Balance Sheet do not even have a resale value. (On the other hand, of course, there is also the possibility that the business possesses real estate which has appreciated in value, and this may fetch amounts substantially higher than the book value).

An owner, whose personal investment in the business is substantial, is likely to be more committed to its success and more involved in its running.

B owes outsiders 750. If the assets fetch a price lower than 750, which is quite likely, the creditors of the organization may not be able to recover their money.

A, on the other hand, owes outsiders only 250. Even if the assets can be disposed of at one fourth the book value, the lenders will be able to recover all their dues.

Balance Sheet A

Liabilities		Assets	
Share Capital	450	Fixed Assets	750
Reserves & Surplus	300		
Long-Term Loans	200	Current Assets	250
Creditors	50		
	1,000		**1,000**

Balance Sheet B

Liabilities		Assets	
Share Capital	150	Fixed Assets	750
Reserves & Surplus	100		
Long-Term Loans	650	Current Assets	250
Creditors	100		
	1,000		**1,000**

Although I may have over-simplified matters a bit, I gave you this example only to show you that, whether or not you realize it, you already know to a certain extent how to read a Balance Sheet!

Reading a Balance Sheet from the Rule II perspective

Let us now understand Rule II and in the process also learn how to read a balance sheet.

So far you have seen that in a typical Balance Sheet there are four items on the left and two on the right as shown here.

Balance Sheet

Liabilities	Assets
Share Capital	Fixed Assets
Reserves & Surplus	
Long-Term Loans	Current Assets
Current Liabilities	

Instead of Current Assets on one side of the Balance Sheet and Current Liabilities on the other, you will often see **Net Current Assets** that is, Current Assets less Current Liabilities, appearing on the Assets' side of the Balance Sheet. These are also called **Net Working Capital**. I will explain this in the next chapter.

Balance Sheets are actually made up of far more numbers than you see here. But to make Balance Sheets easier to read and more meaningful, many items are clubbed together and reduced to six headings, four on one side and two on the other. It is possible that you will come across a Balance Sheet which has numerous items on each side. Don't get confused. If you study each of them you will find that they can all be classified under one of these headings.

An example of a Balance Sheet detailing the different items under the six heads is shown at the end of this chapter.

If you wish to read a Balance Sheet make sure it has not more than four items on the Liabilities' side and not more than two on the Assets'.

Can you now reduce the left hand side to two numbers?

Let's try and reduce the number of items on the Liabilities' side also to two.

How do we do that?
Let's look for similarities between items on the Liabilities' side which can be clubbed together.

There are various possibilities.
Should we combine the first two items (Share Capital and Reserves) and the last two items (Long-Term Loans and Current Liabilities)?

This would give us two items, the first of which represent owners' contribution, and the second funds provided by outsiders. However, this classification is not going to help us read Balance Sheets any better.

A better way would be to club the first three items.
All of these, Share Capital, Reserves & Surplus, as well as Long-Term Loans, represent long-term funds (LTF) or **long-term sources (LTS)**.

Let us see if this is correct.
- Is Share Capital a long-term source?
  Share Capital is for the longest term. It does not have to be repaid in the lifetime of the company.
- What about Reserves?
  Reserves are often as long term as share capital. Even though reserves can be used to distribute as dividends in the years when the company makes losses, this provision is rarely used. If reserves are used at all, it is often to distribute bonus shares – that is, shares which are issued free of cost – amongst the existing shareholders. When this is done, the amount gets transferred from the head reserves to the head share capital.
- Finally, the Long-Term Loans are obviously long term in nature.

Balance Sheet

Liabilities		Assets	
Share Capital	} LTS	Fixed Assets	LTU
Reserves & Surplus			
Long-Term Loans		Current Assets	STU
Current Liabilities	STS		

We can safely say that current liabilities are **short-term sources (STS)**, since an item is classified as a current liability only if it has to be repaid within one year from the date of the Balance Sheet.

Similarly, on the Assets' side, we would not be wrong in saying that Fixed Assets represent **long term uses** of funds (**LTU**), being made up of items such as land and building and machinery and equipment, all of which are purchased for use over the long term.

The current assets, which represent gross working capital, can likewise be called a **short term use** of money (**STU**). In fact the movement of items of current assets (comprising cash, inventory and debtors) can be depicted in the form of a cycle as shown here.

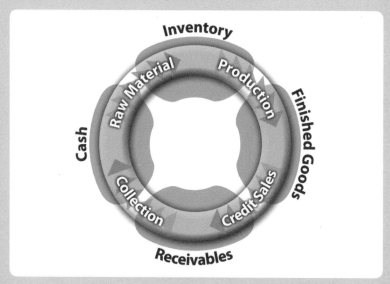

Working Capital Cycle

In the case of a manufacturing organization, cash is used to purchase inventory.

The inventory then goes through a manufacturing process and gets converted to a finished product.

When a sale is made, the finished-goods inventory becomes debtors or receivables.

On the due date, when collection is made from debtors, it gets converted to cash again. This cycle of **cash-to-cash** is called the working-capital cycle.

Profitable organizations know that the key to success is to have a shorter working-capital cycle. Every attempt must be made to shorten this cycle.

An organization that
- keeps inventory at a **three-month** consumption level,
- takes **one month** to convert it to a finished product,
- keeps a finished-goods inventory of another **one month**
- and then sells the product on a **three-month** credit to customers, will have a working-capital cycle of eight months and be able to obtain 1.5 rotations in a year.

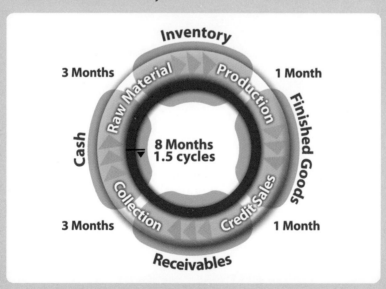

On the other hand, an organization that
- keeps inventory equal to **one month**, (by making sales and production forecasts and an inventory-need analysis and arriving at optimum inventory)
- cuts down the production time to **15 days** (at the same time applying quality-control measures to ensure that hastening production does not compromise quality),
- reduces the finished-goods inventory also to **15 days**,
- and then sells their product on **30 days**' credit (realizing that period of credit is not the only criterion considered by customers while making a purchase, and that customers also take into account product quality, pre-sales and after-sales service, and if necessary, by offering customers a small discount) can bring down the cycle to three months, thereby achieving four cycles in a year, leading to a higher turnover with the same investment as in the first case and consequently far higher profits.

> Profitable organizations know that the key to success is to have a shorter working-capital cycle.

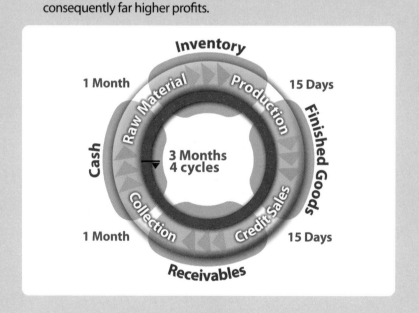

For the limited purpose of our discussion, however, it does not matter whether money comes back in 3 months or 8 months. When an investment gets converted to cash in less than one year, it is called short term.

The new look of the Balance Sheet which has been brought down to two items on the left and two on the right will be as shown here:

Balance Sheet*

Liabilities	Assets
Long-Term Sources (LTS) (comprising Share Capital, Reserves & Surplus and Long Term Loans)	**Long-Term Uses (LTU)** (made up of Fixed Assets)
Short-Term Sources (STS) (comprising Current Liabilities)	**Short-Term Uses (STU)** (represented by Current Assets)

You are now ready to read Balance Sheets.

There are only three types of Balance Sheets

If you now take a large number of Balance Sheets, and present them as having two items on the Sources' side (LTS and STS) and two items on the Uses' side (LTU and STU), **you will discover that all Balance Sheets must fit into one of only three types.**

Every Balance Sheet has three possibilities, and can only be of Type A, Type B or Type C, as depicted on the next page.

---

* For this discussion, we will call a liability repayable within one year as a Short-Term Source. If the liability is to be paid back later than one year it will be classified as Long Term. Similarly, assets which can get liquidated or re-converted into cash within one year will be considered as Short-Term Uses. Those which will not are Long Term.

Take a close look at the three statements.

Balance Sheet A

Liabilities		Assets	
LTS	80	LTU	80
STS	20	STU	20
	100		**100**

Balance Sheet B

Liabilities		Assets	
LTS	90	LTU	80
STS	10	STU	20
	100		**100**

Balance Sheet C

Liabilities		Assets	
LTS	70	LTU	80
STS	30	STU	20
	100		**100**

You might be thinking that there are surely any number of combinations besides those shown here. So what do I mean when I say that these are the only three types of Balance Sheets possible?

To understand this classification, it is essential that you read the statements horizontally and not vertically.

You will then realize that the actual numbers don't matter.

A Balance Sheet is Type A when the long-term sources and the long-term uses match, and the short-term sources and short-term uses also match. It does not matter whether the numbers are 80:20 as in this example, or whether they are 70:30 or 60:40. If the long-term sources amount to 70 and the long-term uses are also 70, if the short-term sources are 30 and the short-term uses are 30, we will call it a Type A Balance Sheet.

A Balance Sheet is Type B when the long-term sources are more than the long-term uses, in which case the short-term sources will be less than the short-term uses.

Finally, when the long-term sources are less than the long-term uses, and consequently the short-term sources are more than the short-term uses, the Balance Sheet will be called Type C.

It is easy to identify Balance Sheets with just two-digit numbers as shown here. In real life you are more likely to come across Balance Sheets with much larger numbers. So let me give you another set of three Balance Sheets to make sure you have understood how to classify them.

Balance Sheet: Example 1

Liabilities		Assets	
LTS	4,752	LTU	5,154
STS	2,598	STU	2,196
	7,350		**7,350**

Balance Sheet: Example 2

Liabilities		Assets	
LTS	11,670	LTU	11,670
STS	3,750	STU	3,750
	15,420		**15,420**

Balance Sheet: Example 3

Liabilities		Assets	
LTS	6,450	LTU	5,460
STS	3,300	STU	4,290
	9,750		**9,750**

Can you examine and assess whether they are Type A, B, or C?

As you will recognize, in the first example the long-term sources are less than the long-term uses and the short-term sources are more than the short-term uses, which make it a Type C Balance Sheet. The second one is Type A and the last is Type B.

Try and get live examples of Balance Sheets and apply this thinking to them. You'll soon find yourself easily able to classify any Balance Sheet you wish to read in this manner.

How would we describe
A, B and C Balance Sheets?

In the three Balance Sheets shown earlier, how should we describe each one?

Balance Sheet A

Liabilities		Assets	
LTS	80	LTU	80
STS	20	STU	20
	100		**100**

A has 80 long-term sources and 80 long-term uses.
A's short-term sources are 20 and so are its short-term uses.

This indicates that A has utilized its long-term funds to acquire long-term assets and short-term funds to finance short-term uses.

Balance Sheet B

Liabilities		Assets	
LTS	90	LTU	80
STS	10	STU	20
	100		**100**

B, on the other hand, has 90 long-term sources but only 80 long-term uses. It appears that B has used long-term funds for long-term purposes and after doing so still has a surplus of long-term funds to the extent of 10.
However on the short-term front, the funds available are 10, but the utilization in short-term investments is to the tune of 20. This deficit has apparently been bridged through diversion of long-term funds.

B, therefore, can be described as having used a part of its long-term funds for short-term purposes.

Balance Sheet C

Liabilities		Assets	
LTS	70	LTU	80
STS	30	STU	20
	100		**100**

C has long-term sources of 70 and long-term uses of 80, showing a deficit. Even if all long-term funds have been used for long-term purposes, C is still running short of 10.
However, since short-term sources are 30 but short-term uses only 20, there is a surplus. In this case, short-term funds of the value of 10 have been diverted for long-term purposes.

C seems to be one who has used some short-term funds for long-term purposes.

All this is just a factual description of what these Balance Sheets reveal.

Which Balance Sheet is the healthiest?

The question now is, which of the three is following sound financial management policies?

Don't forget that we are still trying to understand the application of Rule II.
Rule II reminds us that sources of funds are eventually liabilities.
All who have lent money are going to expect it back. It's only a matter of time.
Prudence must, therefore, be exercised at all times while deploying those resources to ensure that the assets can generate an inflow before the liabilities have to be repaid.

At the same time, it's essential to recognize that some liabilities have to be paid back earlier than others. Those liabilities which we have classified as short-term sources will have to be repaid in the immediate future – over the next few weeks or months, but not later than one year. This is the reason why we isolated the short-term sources and clubbed the rest as long-term sources.

Let's examine the three Balance Sheets again from this perspective.

Take a look at Balance Sheet C.
Who is going to come knocking at C's doors in the near future asking for the money back?
The short-term lenders, of course, which amount to 30.
To repay these, which assets on the right hand side can be liquidated at short notice?
You will easily see that the long-term uses, which are represented by fixed assets, must never be liquidated.
No healthy organization will ever purchase machinery or buildings to sell! These are purchased for use in the business.
The only assets which will bring in cash, in the short run, are the short-

term assets. This happens through the movement of the working-capital cycle, where cash will become cash each time the cycle goes round.

C is expected to repay 30 in the near future, but has only 20 in short-term assets.
In order to meet its short-term liabilities, C will now be forced to sell some long-term assets.
If a business has to sell its fixed assets, its buildings and machinery and equipment, it would jeopardize its very existence.

When an organization is forced to sell its long-term assets in order to meet its short-term liabilities, to me it represents the beginning of the end of that organization.

C is in serious trouble.
And why is C in trouble? This is because it is guilty of using short-term funds for long-term purposes.

That leaves us with A and B.

Let me now give you the rule for a healthy organization. Healthy organizations will ensure that they use their long-term funds for long-term purposes and short-term funds for short-term purposes.

> If a business has to sell its fixed assets, its buildings and machinery and equipment, it would jeopardize its very existence.

As per this rule A should be the healthiest. But that is not so. And I am not saying this because A seems to have the exact value of short-term assets as its short-term liabilities, and could just be cutting it a bit fine.

In fact A, having neither more nor less, is on the right side of our mantra "less is bad, more is worse" and appears to be the epitome of efficiency.

There is another, different, reason for which I believe that A is not the healthiest. A is definitely better than C, but B is even better than A.

In Balance Sheet A, who is expecting to get paid over a short period of time?
The short-term liabilities, which amount to 20.
And how much does A have in the form of short-term assets?
Also 20.

However, do you recall the break-up of short-term assets, which are also known as current assets?
Current assets are made up of cash and bank balances, debtors and inventory.

Balance Sheet A

Liabilities		Assets	
STS	20	STU	20

- Cash
- Debtors
- Inventory

When it is time to pay the short-term liabilities, can A use the cash and bank balances to pay them?
Of course. This is money that is readily available.

And can A use debtors?
Yes, I do think A can use its debtors.
Debtors are parties from whom you have to collect. Creditors are those that you have to pay. Let's put them at par. You can collect from your debtors and use the money to pay off your creditors.
You will doubtless have to use some skill in doing this, and fine-tune your cash flow and perhaps use temporary recourse to a bank overdraft or similar arrangement to deal with the gaps between the dates of collection and dates of payment.

So cash and bank balances can be used to pay short-term liabilities.

> You will doubtless have to ...fine-tune your cash flow and perhaps use temporary recourse to a bank overdraft or similar arrangement to deal with the gaps between the dates of collection and dates of payment.

Debtors can also be used.
But can inventory be used to pay creditors (which make up a substantial portion of current liabilities)?

Before you answer this question, first consider who exactly these creditors are.
A large component of creditors (on the Liabilities' side) will comprise raw-material suppliers.
And inventory (on the Assets' side) represents the stock of raw material.

Using inventory to pay creditors is akin to approaching a vendor for supply of raw material, and when the vendor asks for payment, offering to return the raw material instead of giving money!
No business organization purchases raw material just to return it back to the vendor. Raw Material is purchased so that after going through the production process, it can get converted to finished products.
The finished products will then be sold to customers and get converted to debtors. And when debtors pay up, the money will be used to pay the creditors.

So, since inventory cannot be used to pay creditors, it is obvious that A is not going to have sufficient funds to meet its short-term liabilities.

This brings me to a key accounting ratio called the Current Ratio.

The short-term uses on the Assets' side are current assets. The short-term sources on the Liabilities' side are current liabilities.
The ratio of the two is called the Current Ratio.

Balance Sheet A

Liabilities		Assets		
				Current Ratio
CL	20	CA	20	CA:CL = **1:1**

Balance Sheet B

Liabilities		Assets		
				Current Ratio
CL	10	CA	20	CA:CL = **2:1**

Balance Sheet C

Liabilities		Assets		
				Current Ratio
CL	30	CA	20	CA:CL = **1:1.5**

Healthy companies must try and maintain a Current Ratio (CA:CL) in the region of 2:1.

The problem with A is that its Current Ratio is 1:1.
The Current Ratio of C is 1:1.5.
The Current Ratio in the case of B is exactly what it should be, namely 2:1.

Is it possible for B to get into trouble despite having the perfect Current Ratio?

B's Current Ratio is as per the norm of healthy companies.
However in certain situations B can also develop cash-flow problems.

B's short-term liabilities are 10 and its short-term assets are 20.

As we have seen, short-term assets consist of cash, debtors and inventory.

In financial jargon, cash and debtors are called **liquid current assets** (or quick assets).
Inventory is called a **non-liquid current asset**.

For B to be able to meet its current liabilities on time, you can see that it should possess an equal amount, or more, of liquid current assets.

This brings me to another key ratio, the Quick Ratio (also called the Acid-Test Ratio).

If you break up current assets into those that are liquid and those that are not, the ratio of liquid current assets (LCA) to current liabilities (CL) is called the Quick Ratio.

Balance Sheet B

Liabilities		Assets	
CL	10	CA	20

Cash
Debtors } Quick Assets or Liquid CA
Inventory — Non Liquid CA

Healthy companies will ensure that the Quick Ratio is always maintained at a minimum of 1:1.

If the Current Ratio falls below 2:1, it may not be an immediate cause for alarm. But for the Quick Ratio to fall below 1:1 is a very serious matter.

So B, in order to remain in a position to meet all its current commitments, must ensure that it possesses a minimum of 10 in the form of liquid current assets, that is, in the form of cash plus debtors.
This also means that it can maintain a maximum inventory of 10.
If B's inventory is higher than 10, it will mean that, though it has a good Current Ratio, it is still incapable of meeting its short-term commitments.

To sum up: Healthy organizations must maintain a **Current Ratio** of about **2:1** and a **Quick Ratio** of a minimum of **1:1**.

If the Current Ratio falls below 2:1, it may not be an immediate cause for alarm.
But for the Quick Ratio to fall below 1:1 is a very serious matter, and if corrective measures are not urgently taken, it can lead to situations of financial insolvency.

What are the lessons that we can learn from this example?

The lessons gleaned from understanding Rule II can be summed up as follows:

Healthy organizations

should use long-term funds for long-term purposes and short-term funds for short-term purposes.

may use, or rather should use, some long-term funds for short-term purposes.

But should NEVER use short-term funds for long-term purposes.

Healthy companies must maintain

a Current Ratio of about 2:1

a Liquid Ratio of minimum 1:1

EXAMPLE OF A BALANCE SHEET
DETAILING DIFFERENT ITEMS UNDER THE SIX MAIN HEADS

BALANCE SHEET

Liabilities	Assets
SHARE CAPITAL	**FIXED ASSETS**
Authorized Capital Issued Capital Subscribed Capital Paid-up Capital	Buildings, Plant & Machinery, Furniture & Fixtures, Vehicles
RESERVES & SURPLUS	
General Reserve Capital Reserve Asset Replacement Reserve Dividend Equalization Reserve Profit & Loss Account	
LONG-TERM LOANS	
SECURED	
Debentures Loan from Financial Institutions Bank Borrowings Other Loans	
UNSECURED	
Public Deposits Inter-Corporation Deposits Commercial Paper Interest Free Sales-Tax Loan	
CURRENT LIABILITIES	**CURRENT ASSETS**
Bills Payables Deposits from Dealers Interest Accrued	Inventories Debtors Cash & Bank Balances
PROVISIONS	
Proposed Dividends Provisions for Retirement & Other Employee Benefits	

If you wish to learn more about finance management, you can enroll for our

Live & Online Training Sessions

These are highly interactive training sessions covering various topics of Finance Management. These programs are tailor-made to suit your existing business schedules ranging from one and two day seminars to five day workshops.

Dr Anil Lamba

Chartered Accountant,
International Corporate Trainer,
Financial Literacy Activist and
Author of the bestselling book

ROMANCING THE BALANCE SHEET

Call : +91.99 22 351 352
Email : training@lamconschool.com
Website : www.lamconschool.com

LAMCON® | Financial Intelligence for Profitable Growth

124

CHAPTER

9

Net Working Capital

and the 'Credibility Trap'

Examine the role played by Current Assets
and Current Liabilities to arrive at the
Net Working Capital and understand
how to avoid the 'Credibility Trap'

In the previous chapter we touched upon the complexities of working capital and its optimum use. Let's now deepen this understanding with a few more examples and ideas.

Take a look at this Balance Sheet.

Balance Sheet

Liabilities		Assets	
Long-Term Sources	90	Fixed Assets	80
Current Liabilities	10	Current Assets	20
	100		**100**

As you know, the Assets' side of a Balance Sheet reveals where the resources of the organization have been deployed.

Businesses invest money in the creation of **fixed assets** like land, buildings, machinery and equipment, furniture and fixtures.

They also require a continuous supply of **working capital** so that, in addition to acquiring fixed assets, they can:
- purchase and maintain an inventory of raw material
- hold on to sufficient cash in hand, so that day-to-day expenses, salaries, overheads and so on can be met
- afford to continue production at great cost to themselves, and then sell it to customers without demanding to be paid upfront.

Working capital requirement is thus the sum total of the money needed by enterprises to maintain inventory, hold on to a certain minimum cash balance, and also be able to finance customers in the sense that when goods are sold on credit, the organization effectively assumes the role of financier to the customer, lending goods instead of money.

Current assets, however, represent what is known as **Gross Working Capital**.

You may also be familiar with the expression **Net Working Capital**.

Net Working Capital is calculated as **Gross Working Capital less Current Liabilities**.

Gross Working Capital = **Current Assets**

Net Working Capital = **Current Assets**
(−) Current Liabilities

In the Balance Sheet we have just looked at, the gross working capital requirement is 20.
But the net working capital requirement is only 10 (CA 20 less CL 10).

> Just as debtors represent the need for working capital, creditors represent the extent to which it was possible to meet the requirement of working capital without having to pay for it.

How did the gross requirement of working capital of 20 reduce to a net requirement of 10?

As per the formula, when there are current liabilities on a Balance Sheet, it results in a reduction of the working capital requirement.

This happens because current liabilities represent the extent to which the organization was able to procure the goods and services it needed without having to pay for them immediately. These would be the goods and services purchased on credit.

Just as debtors (on the Assets' side) represent the need for working capital, creditors represent the extent to which it was possible to meet the requirement of working capital without having to pay for it.

And net working capital (CA – CL) is the amount of money the organization will have to actually invest to sustain its current assets. This difference comes from long-term sources.

In the example given above, the total long-term sources are 90, of which 80 were used to acquire fixed assets and 10 to finance the net working capital requirement.

The Credibility Trap

As you have just seen, current liabilities play the role of reducing the working capital required to finance current assets.

Out of a total current-assets' requirement of 20, the organization managed to procure 10 on credit. So it needed an infusion of only 10 from long-term sources.

If however, the organization had enjoyed a higher credibility amongst suppliers and vendors, perhaps it would have been possible to obtain credit to the extent of 15, in which case the net working capital requirement would have dropped further to 5.

And, if the organization was able to command 20 (due to an immensely high standing), the need for working capital would disappear, and the organization would be functioning fully on others' money.

It follows, therefore, that the greater the credibility that a firm enjoys, the lower would be its net working capital requirement.

However, there is a trap in this.

As current liabilities keep increasing, the working capital ratio becomes successively worse.

Take a look at these three Balance Sheets.

Balance Sheet — I

Liabilities		Assets		NWC	CR
CL	10	CA	20	10	2:1

Balance Sheet — II

Liabilities		Assets		NWC	CR
CL	15	CA	20	5	1.33:1

Balance Sheet — III

Liabilities		Assets		NWC	CR
CL	20	CA	20	Nil	1:1

In case I the Current Ratio (CR) was 2:1, in case II it fell to 1.33:1 and to 1:1 in case III.
We know, however, that healthy organizations must maintain a current ratio of about 2:1.

In the case we have just seen, had the current liabilities been 25, the firm would have a negative Net Working Capital (NWC).

This is what I refer to as the **Credibility Trap**.

Organizations with a bad current ratio are not necessarily 'bad organizations' but they are 'entrapped organizations'; where those in charge of running them did not understand the principles of good financial management.

So where's the trap?

Earlier, while discussing Rule II of Good Financial Management, we have seen that all Balance Sheets can be classified into three types, A, B and C.

The C type Balance Sheet (reproduced here), which we had concluded was in a very precarious and vulnerable position, had a negative working capital.
It had current liabilities of 30 as against current assets of 20.

Balance Sheet C

Liabilities		Assets	
LTS	70	LTU	80
STS Current Liabilities	30	STU Current Assets	20
	100		**100**

The mere fact that C has a negative working capital does not necessarily make it a bad company.

It could even be a wonderful firm, with immense credibility. Because of this, C may have been able to raise short-term resources to the tune of 30, even though it only needed 20.

The trap lies in the fact that whenever an organization has more short-term resources than it can absorb in short-term avenues, it is only natural that those resources will be utilised for long-term purposes, and this would be a big mistake.

As current liabilities keep increasing, the working capital ratio becomes successively worse.

Because this is a wonderful company, because it is immensely successful, because it is constantly growing and expanding, there will always be projects which are at various stages of completion. From time to time these projects will slow down when resources are scarce.

When such an organization finds that on the one hand its projects are starved of money, and, on the other, there is excess money available in the short-term resources, it would be almost impossible to prevent the managers from using these resources for their long-term projects.

What is worse is that often, in such cases, the perpetrators of the crime may not even be aware of the consequences of their action.
They could be totally ignorant that short-term funds are being used for long-term purposes. To know and understand this, good Management Information Systems need to be in place, meaningful reports need to be regularly generated, ratios need to be constantly monitored, and those in charge need to be trained to read and understand financial reports. It often happens that the information generated is either inadequate or too late to be of any use.

This organization will now become guilty of one of the worst crimes in financial mismanagement and that is the use of short-term sources for long-term purposes.

When I was young
I used to think that money
was the most important
thing in life.
Now that I am old,
I know it is.

Oscar Wilde
(1854-1900)
Irish Playwright, Poet and Author

CHAPTER 10

Trading on Equity
How to use Fixed-Cost Assets or Funds to Magnify Returns

Understand the financial implications of raising funds through a combination of equity and debt, and how it is possible to take a look at the top line and understand the bottom line

Organizations often make a public offering of shares to raise capital. Through this, they invite members of the public to invest in the organization. Those who do so are called shareholders.

If you are approached by an organization to invest in its shares, on what basis would you make a decision? There would surely be several questions you would want answered before you made up your mind. These questions would pertain to the product or service offered, the organization's future prospects, its past track record, the credibility of its management team, its past stock market performance, its credit rating, and so on.

But what if two organizations approach you with the opportunity to invest and they are identical on each of the above parameters?

Both operate in the same domain, their future prospects appear as bright, each one's track record is as impressive, and the managements are equally credible.

They are alike in all respects but one.

The only area of difference is in their approach towards the source from which they plan to raise the money.
Typically, businesses are funded through a combination of equity and debt.
One of these organizations believes in raising a larger quantum of funds from equity.
The other prefers to borrow more.

This is the only difference.

Once the funds are raised, both companies would invest them in an identical fashion.
They would purchase similar infrastructure, hire an identical number of people, make the same product, sell the same quantity and make the same amount of profit.

Take a look at this table:

Statement showing Capital Employed

	A	B
Equity Shares of 100 each	1500,000	500,000
10% Loan	500,000	1500,000
= Capital Employed	2 000,000	2 000,000

Both A and B need a total investment of two million.

A raises 1.5 million through an equity share issue and a half million through debt which carries an interest rate of 10 percent per annum. In the case of B, half a million comes from equity and the balance 1.5 million from debt.

Have you picked the one you prefer? Is it A or B?

Now let's try to find out who is going to be better off.

As I said earlier, both companies are identical, even to the extent of the profits they earn.

But let me make sure you are clear in your mind about what exactly profit is.

The process of earning profits begins with Sales.
From the Sales figure, we deduct the direct cost (cost of sales), to arrive at the Gross Profit.

We now deduct indirect costs too, to arrive at the Operating Profit or PBIT (profit before interest and tax).
This is the stage of profit where we have recovered from the sales income all direct and indirect cost, but have not yet paid interest to the lender, income tax to the government, or dividends to the shareholder.

From PBIT we first pay interest, and are left with PBT or profit before tax.

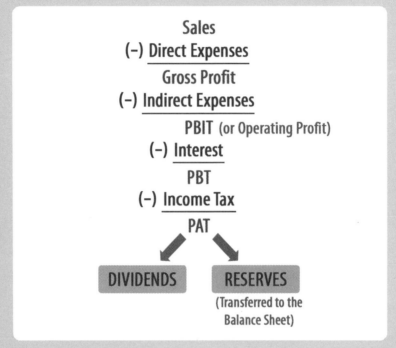

The government must now receive its due. Deducting taxes from PBT we are left with PAT (profit after tax).
PAT belongs to the shareholders or owners of the organization.

As you know, the entire amount of profit after tax is usually not distributed among the shareholders.
There are various reasons for this, one being the fact that profit does not mean money. To distribute dividends, an organization needs money.

As a result, only a portion of the profit gets distributed by way of dividends, and the remainder is retained within the organization.
This remainder appears on the Liabilities' side as **Reserves & Surplus**.

Which of these figures do you think the shareholder is most interested in?

Though you might imagine that the shareholder is more interested in dividends, a prudent investor would actually be happier with a healthy PAT.

When an organization earns an impressive PAT, the shareholders may either receive large dividends, which would naturally make them happy, or a bigger component may be transferred to reserves – and this could make them even happier.

This is because when reserves increase, the net worth of the shareholder goes up. Consequently the book value of the shares also goes up, and this can result in stock-market appreciation of the value of the shares. Often, the gain through market appreciation is far more than the dividend the shareholder would have received.

> They have identical businesses. Why then are the owners of one taking home a 150 percent higher return than the owners of the other business?

A and B are identical companies.
But to what extent will they remain identical?
Their sales will be the same, and so will the direct expenses and therefore their gross profit.
Their indirect expenses and their PBIT figures will also be the same.
But here the similarity must come to an end.
The interest obligations will vary as they have borrowed differently.

Since the similarity between A and B ends at the PBIT, any comparison between the two can begin not later than the PBIT stage.

Let's assume that both are generating a PBIT on capital employed at the rate of 30 percent.

Take a look at this table.

Statement showing calculation of PAT

	A	B
Equity Shares of 100 each	1 500,000	500,000
10% Loan	500,000	1 500,000
= Capital Employed	**2 000,000**	**2 000,000**
PBIT (@30%)	600,000	600,000
(-) Interest	50,000	150,000
= PBT	550,000	450,000
(-) Income Tax (assumed @40%)	220,000	180,000
= PAT	**330,000**	**270,000**

On the face of it, it appears that even though A and B have invested identical sums in their businesses, are running businesses with identical turnovers and expenses, the PAT (the profit that belongs to the owners) in the case of A is higher than in the case of B.

Now look at the earnings per share. This is calculated as PAT divided by the total number of shares.

	A	B
$\dfrac{\text{PAT}}{\text{Number of Shares}}$	$\dfrac{330,000}{15,000}$	$\dfrac{270,000}{5,000}$
= EPS (Earning Per Share)	**22**	**54**

You will see that A has an EPS of 22, but B's EPS is 54!

Even though B earns a lower PAT in absolute terms, you can see that it enjoys a substantially higher EPS.

In other words, the owners of A have invested 1500,000 and earned 330,000, translating into a return on shareholders' capital of 22 percent.
In the case of B the percentage return on an investment of 500,000 works out to 54.

The question that begs for an answer is: **WHY?**

Two organizations have launched identical businesses, with similar investment outlays. They make and sell similar products, at the same selling prices, with costs of manufacturing, selling and administration which are also the same. Why then are the owners of one taking home a 150 percent higher return than the owners of the other business?

It's not that one makes tables and the other software. Either both are making tables, or both are making software.
It's not that one runs a hundred-room hotel and the other has two hundred rooms. Both have either one hundred or two hundred rooms.

Then why should the two earn differently?

> Owners' money is the most expensive source of money. Borrowed funds are relatively cheaper.

The focus of any business enterprise should be on maximizing returns for the owners.
Many believe that profit is the automatic result of the ability to make and the ability to sell.
If this was true, then shouldn't two organizations with identical capabilities to make and sell also have the same profits?

Let's now find some answers.

There are three reasons why B earns so much more than A.

The first reason

The first reason is one that we have discussed at length while explaining Rule I of good financial management. A and B are identical as far as costs of manufacture, sales, and administration are concerned. The difference lies in the cost of funding.

A's business is funded primarily using owners' money.
B, on the other hand, has taken a substantial portion of the required funds from borrowed sources.

As we saw during our discussion of Rule I, owners' money is the most expensive source of money. Borrowed funds are relatively cheaper.

In the case of A, 75 percent of the total funds have come from shareholders or owners, while B has taken only 25 percent from this expensive source, and 75 percent has come from a cheaper source. This makes B's average cost of capital substantially lower than A's.

The PBIT generated is at the rate of 30 percent. In B's case this means that B earns 30 percent on 500,000 raised from shareholders. But B also earns 30 percent on the borrowed 1500,000, on which it is obliged to pay just 10 percent. This difference of 20 percent also goes straight into B's pocket. B therefore earns for its shareholders 30 percent on 500,000 (shareholders' contribution) as well as 20 percent on 1500,000 (the borrowed investment), taking, in the process, the return on shareholders' funds substantially higher.

The second reason

To understand the second reason we must first understand the difference between the costs of borrowing and owners' funds.

If you look at the profitability statement in the example we just discussed, and observe the order in which the costs of borrowed funds and owners' funds appear, you will notice that the interest (cost of borrowing) appears first, before the payment of tax,

> Interest is pre-tax but dividends are post-tax. Interest is a tax-deductible item and dividends are paid out of after-tax profits.

and the dividends (cost of owners' money), are paid from profits after tax. In other words interest is pre-tax but dividends are post-tax. Interest is a tax-deductible item and dividends are paid out of after-tax profits.

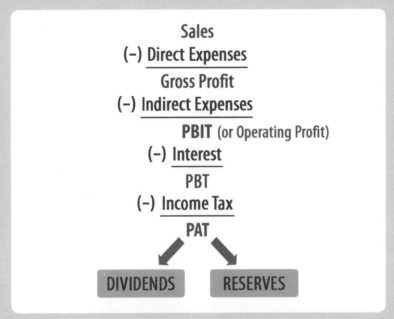

So what impact does this have?

In this example, if B did not have to pay 150,000 towards interest, do you think the take-home profit for the shareholders would be higher by 150,000?
It would not.
The reason this would not happen is because if B did not pay the interest, the Profit Before Tax (PBT) figure would be higher by 150,000. In that case B would have to pay higher income tax to the tune of 40 percent of this amount, and the take-home profit for B's shareholders would be higher only to the extent of 60 percent of 150,000.

In other words, whenever an organization resorts to cost-cutting or economizing and manages to spend, say, 100 less on any item that is tax deductible (such as salary, raw materials, business overheads or interest), the result is that the PBT increases by 100. Consequently the tax liability increases by 40, and the bottom line gets positively impacted only to the extent of 60.

By saving 100, the organization gains only an additional 60. Conversely, by spending 100 extra, the organization pays, out of its own pocket, only 60.

Who pays the remaining 40? The government.

Whenever the government permits an item to be tax-deductible, it is effectively saying, "Go ahead and spend liberally. For every 100 that you spend, you put in 60 and we will contribute 40" assuming a tax rate of 40 percent. If the tax rate was higher or lower, the government's contribution would be correspondingly higher or lower.

Interest is tax-deductible, dividend is not.

We know that at 10 percent, interest is substantially cheaper than owners' capital.

What we now realize is that interest is not only cheap but also tax-deductible, which makes it even cheaper!

The effective rate of interest works out to 6 percent (60 percent of 10 percent).

B has earned a PBIT at the rate of 30 percent not only on its investment of 500,000 but also on the borrowed component of 1500,000, on which it is obliged to pay an effective rate of 6 percent.

B consequently earns for itself 30 percent of 500,000 and 24 percent (30 – 6) of 1500,000 too, taking, in the process, the return on shareholders' funds shooting skywards!

The third reason

To understand the third reason, you need to first understand a very important concept in Finance called the **leverage effect**.

Most CEOs, managing directors and senior managers of an organization are usually aware, sometimes on an on-line basis, of their sales turnover figures, or the top line.

But the black hole is the bottom line.

I have known owners and CEOs who are so much in the dark that they would not know whether the organization has made a profit or a loss unless the accountant completes the accounting process and prepares a Profit & Loss Account.

I find this dependence on accounting and clerical staff alarming.

I have often wondered what would happen if the accountant, or for that matter the typist, was to erroneously type a zero or two more or less. Would the CEO, so dependent on clerks and typists, base all subsequent decisions on the data so provided?

In my opinion responsible business heads must have tools and techniques at their disposal with the help of which, merely by looking at the top line, they can gauge the bottom line with a fair degree of accuracy.

In this chapter and the next, let me show you some such techniques.

For this, I must explain the concept of leverage, and in the process give you the third reason why B makes more profit.

How to look at the top line and understand the bottom line

Suppose your sales turnover last year was 100 and your profit was 20. This year, you are monitoring your top line, and you are aware that your sales is 200. Can you guess the profit made this year?

	Year 1	Year 2
Sales	100	200
Profit	20	?

There are only three possibilities.
The profit can be 40, or it can be less than 40, or more than 40.
Which, according to you, is more likely?
If the turnover has doubled do you expect the profit to double?
Or will it be less than double?
Or more than double?

If you estimated profit to be more than 40, I would agree.

If sales doubled but profits less-than-doubled, in my opinion, some heads should roll. Somebody has been bungling up badly!

If sales doubled but profits less-than-doubled, in my opinion, some heads should roll. Somebody has been bungling up badly!

If you agree that when sales of 100 in year 1 doubles to 200 in year 2, then profit will more than double to beyond 40, let me ask a question.
How much more than 40 can the profit be?
Can profit in the second year increase to 60? Or 80? Or 100? Or even 120?

Yes, all of these ARE possible.

	Year 1	Year 2				
		Option 1	Option 2	Option 3	Option 4	Option 5
Sales	100	200	200	200	200	200
Profit	20	40	60	80	100	120

Of the five options shown, two are remote possibilities, while the other three are realistic.

In year 2, profit growing to 40 (option 1) is as unlikely – though theoretically possible – as to 120 (option 5).

The reality will lie somewhere in between.

Let me explain.

The logic is actually very simple. When sales is 100 and profit is 20, what this means is that the cost is 80.

Now when sales double to 200, when can profit of 20 double to 40? Only when the cost of 80 also doubles to 160.

Option 1	Year 1	Year 2
Sales	100	200
Cost	80	160
Profit	20	40

How likely is this? Not very.
As you can imagine, not all costs are going to double.

Certain heads of expense like raw-material consumption and commission on sales may well double. But there are many other expenses that would either remain the same or increase only marginally.

Since costs will less-than-double, profits will more-than-double.

The other extreme we are considering is of the profit increasing to 120. The sales have increased from 100 to 200.
The profit of 20 can increase to 120 only when the costs of 80 remain 80.

Option 5	Year 1	Year 2
Sales	100	200
Cost	80	80
Profit	20	120

This is also not likely to happen. All costs cannot remain the same. This shows us that these two options, while possible, are highly unlikely.

Now let's try to understand the impact of an increase in sales on profit

In Year 1, sales was 100 and profit was 20. Where did this data come from?
This information must have been taken from the Profit & Loss Account.

The Profit & Loss Account for year 1 would look something like this.

Profit & Loss Account

Expenses	Yr 1	Incomes	Yr 1
Raw material	45	**Sales**	**100**
Power	4		
Salaries	10		
Commission	5		
Rent	16		
	80		
Profit	20		
	100		100

Now, let's try to answer our question: What would be the profit if sales increased from 100 to 200?

When sales double, what is the possibility that raw material consumption will double?
Yes, it probably will.
What about power? Yes, power consumption and cost will also very likely double.

Now do you think salary will increase to twice as much?
Not likely.

Salary cost may remain at the same level or may go up somewhat on account of annual increments or some additional staff, but it will not double.

Commission will usually double.

Rent would probably remain the same.

If you examine the nature of each head of expense, you will discover that some are variable by nature, while others are fixed. That is, some expenses will increase proportionately with an increase in sales while others will not.

Let's write the letter **V** (for variable) and the letter **F** (for fixed) against every head.

Profit & Loss Account

	Expenses	Yr 1	Yr2	Incomes	Yr1	Yr2
V	Raw material	45	90	Sales	**100**	**200**
V	Power	4	8			
F	Salaries	10	10			
V	Commission	5	10			
F	Rent	16	16			
		80				
	Profit	**20**				
		100			**100**	

Now knowing that when sales is 100, cost is 80 and profit is 20, if you wish to guess the profit on a sale of 200, you would first need to know how the cost of 80 is broken up into variable and fixed costs.

Let us consider five different cases.

	Year 1	Break-up of total cost between variable (V) and fixed (F)				
		Case 1	Case 2	Case 3	Case 4	Case 5
Sales	100					
Cost	80	V 80	V 60	V 40	V 20	V --
		F --	F 20	F 40	F 60	F 80
Profit	20					

In Case 1, let's assume that the total cost of 80 was made up entirely of variable costs and there were no fixed costs.
In Case 2, the total cost of 80 is made up of VC 60 and FC 20.
In Case 3, the VC is 40 and FC is 40.
In Case 4, VC is 20 and FC is 60 and
In Case 5 the entire 80 is fixed cost.

Let's now look at what will happen to profit as the ratio between fixed and variable cost changes.

Case 1:
In this situation, when sales double to 200, costs will double to 160 and profit will also double to 40.
When will profits double if sales were to double?
This will only happen if the entire cost was variable.
This, of course, is not very likely.

Case 2:
If the composition of the total cost was 60 variable and 20 fixed: sales having doubled to 200, the variable component of 60 will double to 120.
However the fixed costs of 20 will remain 20.
This makes the total cost 140. The profit of 20 will now grow to 60.

Case 3:
If the variable component was 40 and fixed 40, then profit will increase to 80.

> Leverage is a name given to a disproportionate change in the bottom line of an organization due to a certain change in the top line.

Case 4:
If the break-up between variable and fixed was 20:60, the profit would increase to 100.

Case 5:
If all costs of 80 were fixed by nature (most unlikely), profit would increase from 20 to 120.

Impact on Profit as the ratio between VC and FC changes

	Year 1	Year 2								
		Case 1		Case 2		Case 3		Case 4		Case 5	
Sales	100		200		200		200		200		200
Cost	80	V 80	160	V 60	120	V 40	80	V 20	40	V --	--
		F --	--	F 20	20	F 40	40	F 60	60	F 80	80
T Cost	80		160		140		120		100		80
Profit	20		40		60		80		100		120

Now I have a question for you.
When do organizations make more profits?
Is it when the fixed costs that they bear are less or more?
Do higher fixed costs mean higher profits?
Or do lower fixed costs lead to higher profits?

Chances are that you will pick the second option.

However the figures in the illustration show that when the fixed cost was zero, the profit increased from 20 in year 1 to only 40 in year 2.
Then, when the fixed costs were 20, the profit increased to 60.
When the fixed costs were 40, the profit went up to 80.
And when the fixed costs were the highest, the impact on profit was the most.
When did profit increase the most?
In the situation where the fixed costs were the highest.
Moral of the story: Higher the fixed costs, higher the profit.

But this doesn't sound quite right!
How can profits increase when fixed costs, or for that matter any costs, increase?

If this is true, then maybe we should just announce that effective tomorrow all salaries will be doubled. This would increase fixed costs, and as per our new mantra, surely the profits would increase too?

Please don't do this, since any arbitrary increase in cost is only going to reduce our profit!
Then what do I mean when I say "Higher the Fixed Costs, Higher the Profit"?

What we do need to do is look a little deeper and try to understand exactly how we can practically apply this dictum.

Let's go back to our example. Consider that the 5 columns showing different cases in the second year reflect the performance of five different companies A, B, C, D, and E.

	Year 1		Year 2								
			A		B		C		D		E
Sales	100		200		200		200		200		200
Cost	80	V 80	160	V 60	120	V 40	80	V 20	40	V --	--
		F --	--	F 20	20	F 40	40	F 60	60	F 80	80
T Cost	80		160		140		120		100		80
Profit	20		40		60		80		100		120

In Year 1, all five companies had a sales turnover of 100, costs of 80, and profits of 20.

The only difference between each one is the composition of their fixed and variable costs.
A had only variable and no fixed costs.

B had a fixed-cost component of 20.
C's fixed cost was 40, D's was 60 and E's was 80.
The following year, all five worked equally hard and managed to double their sales turnovers from 100 to 200.

When A's turnover doubled, profit doubled.
When B's turnover doubled, profit trebled.
In C's case, profit quadrupled.
D's profit quintupled.
In the case of E, profit increased sixfold.

Who had the highest fixed cost? E.
Whose profit increased the most? E's.
Moral of the story:
Higher the Fixed Costs, Higher the Profits.
Then why do I say, "Don't phone your banker and insist that a higher interest be charged on all your loans so that you can increase your Fixed Costs"?

Take a closer look.
It is true that between A, B, C, D and E, with an identical increase in turnover, E's profit increased the most.
It is also true that E had the highest fixed costs.

However, do you notice that the total cost of all five in the first year was 80?
E did not incur higher costs than the others.

The only difference between the five is the composition of total costs. Within the same overall cost of 80, A had the lowest fixed cost and E the highest.

If you increase salaries or rent or interest arbitrarily, costs will increase, and consequently profit will reduce.

Why does Profit increase disproportionately when the Fixed Cost component is higher?

Let me first give you the logic of why there is a disproportionate change in profit when the proportion of fixed costs is higher.

Profit will increase in the same proportion as the change in sales only when all costs are variable by nature.

In such cases, if sales double, costs will double and profit will merely double.

But when costs include an element of fixed cost, when sales double, all costs will not double. The variable cost will increase, but fixed cost will remain fixed. This means that the total cost will less-than-double, and the profit will more-than-double.

This phenomenon, where a one hundred percent increase in sales can lead to a two hundred or three hundred or four hundred percent increase in profit, is called the leverage effect.

Leverage, in this context, is a name given to a disproportionate change in the bottom line of an organization due to a certain change in the top line.
And the leverage effect is caused by the presence of fixed costs in the costing structure.

So the challenge, therefore, is to increase fixed costs without increasing overall costs.

The only way this can be done is by swapping some variable costs with fixed costs.

Which variable costs can be replaced with fixed costs?

All variable costs, obviously, cannot be exchanged with fixed costs. Some costs, such as the cost of raw material, will usually continue to remain variable.

But consider the following situations:

The next time your organization plans to recruit sales and marketing personnel, and is trying to figure out the compensation structure – should it offer a smaller fixed salary and a higher incentive or vice versa?

You must understand that salary is a fixed cost while incentive is variable.

Maybe, as a strategy, you would want to study the industry standards and then announce a salary which is 50 percent higher than the highest in your industry, but without, or with very low, incentives. When you offer such a high salary, you will attract the best talent. This talent will have a positive impact on your top line. This increase in top line has come accompanied by a fixed cost. This will lead to a disproportionate increase in the bottom line.

We should focus on increasing only those fixed costs which can also positively impact the top line. Only when the increased fixed costs lead to an increase in the sales figure will the profit increase disproportionately.

If you are trying to decide whether the new product should be made in-house or whether you should outsource the job, *one of the factors to be taken into account* is that outsourcing involves mainly variable costs, whereas in-house manufacture will contain elements of fixed costs.

To fund your expansion you need to decide whether to raise resources from lenders or whether to make a fresh issue of equity. You must remember that the cost of borrowing (interest) is a fixed cost whereas the cost of owners' money (dividend) is variable. **This, therefore, gives us the third reason why B generates a substantially higher EPS than A.**

Take a look at this table again.

	A	B
Equity Shares of 100 each	1 500,000	500,000
10% Loan	500,000	1 500,000
= **Capital Employed**	**2 000,000**	**2 000,000**
PBIT (@30%)	600,000	600,000
(-) Interest	50,000	150,000
= PBT	550,000	450,000
(-) Income Tax (assumed @40%)	220,000	180,000
= PAT	330,000	270,000
PAT	330,000	270,000
Number of Shares	15,000	5,000
= **EPS**	22	54

Between A and B, who has borrowed more? – B
Who pays more interest? – B
Whose fixed-cost commitment is higher? – B's
Therefore whose EPS is more? – B's

B earns a substantially higher rate of return because of a higher fixed cost in its costing structure. B is committed to pay an annual interest of 150,000 as compared to 50,000 in the case of A, which, at first glance, is horrifying. However this fact has resulted in B having an EPS or Return On Investment (ROI) which is two-and-a-half times that of A.

I must, however, warn you that the strategy of increasing fixed costs to increase profits is only recommended for good times, when markets are booming and the sales graph seems to be moving consistently upward.

> We should focus on increasing only those fixed costs which can also positively impact the top line. Only when the increased fixed costs lead to an increase in the sales figure will the profit increase disproportionately.

When recession sets in, it is time to begin swapping the fixed costs with variable costs wherever possible. This is because when sales drop, the variable costs will also decrease, but the fixed costs will remain fixed. And if the fixed cost component is high it can lead to a drastic and disproportionate fall in profit.

The old foundations of success are gone ...
The world's wealthiest man, Bill Gates, owns nothing tangible: no land, no gold or oil, no factories ...
For the first time in history the world's wealthiest man owns only knowledge.

Lester Thurow
(1938 -)
US Economist, Management Theorist, and Writer

CHAPTER 11

Marginal Costing Principles
& Break-Even Analysis

Apply Marginal Costing principles to
understand your business better, and
to take financially intelligent decisions

For any organization, the usual method of calculating profit is by making a Profit & Loss Account, which lists out the incomes on one side and the numerous items of expense on the other.

As we saw in the previous chapter, when we examine the various heads of expense we find that they can all be classified, by nature, as either **Variable Costs (VC)** or **Fixed Costs (FC)**.
Some of the expenses, however, would be partially variable and partially fixed. These must be segregated, and the variable component added to the VC and the fixed component to the FC.

We then see that profit becomes a function of Sales less the sum of Variable Cost and Fixed Cost.

If you deduct only the Variable Cost from Sales, what you get is called Contribution. And Contribution less Fixed Cost is equal to Profit.

Understanding Contribution

We now have a comprehensive and more meaningful formula for profit:

$$
\begin{array}{rl}
& \text{Sales} \\
(-) & \underline{\text{Variable Cost}} \\
& \text{Contribution} \\
(-) & \underline{\text{Fixed Cost}} \\
& \underline{\text{Profit / (Loss)}}
\end{array}
$$

Let's now try to understand this concept in practical terms.
Imagine that Rita has set up a small furniture-manufacturing business. The main product of this organization is tables.
What would be the most obvious variable cost in the manufacture of wooden furniture?
Yes, raw material, which in this case is wood.

Let's say Rita consumes wood worth 100 in the manufacture of one table.

Now let's think of an example of Rita's fixed cost. Say rent.
Rita pays a rent of 10,000 per month.
Whether she makes one table or ten, the rent will remain 10,000 (till, with an increase in the volume of tables, she feels the need to rent additional space).

If Rita was to make just one table, what would it cost her?
The cost of raw material is 100, and since she makes only one table, the entire fixed cost of 10,000 would have to be absorbed by the single table.
Rita's cost of manufacturing one table would be 10,100.

> As long as Contribution is less than Fixed Cost, businesses make losses. When Contribution equals Fixed Cost, they break even. And it is when Contribution exceeds Fixed Cost, that businesses make profits.

And if Rita wishes to make a profit she would have to sell her table for more than 10,100. Rita, of course, realizes that fixing the selling price is not in her control. Selling price is decided by the market, taking competitors' pricing strategies into consideration. If her competitors are selling similar tables for, say, 250, she is also going to have to price her table at not more than 250.

What would be the bottom line if Rita makes and sells just one table at a selling price of 250?

Quantity	1
Sales	250
(-) Variable Cost	100
= Contribution	150
(-) Fixed Cost	10,000
= Profit / Loss	9,850

At this point of time her business appears to be making a loss of 9,850.

Since she does not wish to make a loss, she comes to you for advice. What would you advice her?

You would doubtless suggest that she increase the number of tables produced and sold.

Heeding your advice, Rita now doubles production to two tables. Let's see how this will affect the bottom line.

Quantity	1	2
Sales	250	500
(-) Variable Cost	100	200
= Contribution	150	300
(-) Fixed Cost	10,000	10,000
= Profit / Loss	9,850	9,700

The loss has now reduced to 9,700.

She then makes the third table, and the loss further drops to 9,550.

Quantity	1	2	3	10
Sales	250	500	750	2,500
(-) Variable Cost	100	200	300	1,000
= Contribution	150	300	450	1,500
(-) Fixed Cost	10,000	10,000	10,000	10,000
= Profit / Loss	9,850	9,700	9,550	8,500

When Rita makes 10 tables, her loss is reduced to 8,500. Rita begins to wonder when her business will break even.

A formula for Break-Even Point

Let's try and create a formula for Break-Even Point, the point at which the business is making neither profit nor loss.

> **The condition necessary to break even is that Contribution must equal Fixed Cost.**

At this point of time, why is the business making a loss? The table shows that Sales minus Variable Cost is Contribution, and Contribution minus Fixed Cost is profit.
The business is making a loss because the amount of Contribution is lower than the amount of Fixed Cost.

But you will observe that as the quantity of tables made increased from 1 to 2 to 3 and then to 10, with each increase in Sales the Contribution also increased.
But the Fixed Cost, being fixed, remained the same.
Table by table, the gap between Contribution and Fixed Cost kept reducing.

It is not difficult to now imagine that as the quantity of tables continues to increase, the Contribution will also consistently increase. And then a stage will come when Contribution will be 10,000. This is the Break-Even Point.

> As long as Contribution is less than Fixed Cost, businesses make losses. When Contribution equals Fixed Cost, they break even. And it is when Contribution exceeds Fixed Cost, that businesses make profits.

Therefore the condition necessary to break even is that Contribution must equal Fixed Cost.

This, then, gives us the formula for break-even point, which is:

$$\text{Break-Even Point} = \frac{\text{Fixed Cost}}{\text{Contribution per unit}}$$

In Rita's case, her fixed cost is 10,000.
Each table generates a Contribution of 150.
This means that she must manufacture and sell 66.66 (that is
10,000/150) tables in order to break even.

The minute she has made and sold her 67th table, she is out of the red!
The 67th table brings her a profit of 50.
And on selling the 68th table, her profit increases to 200.

Quantity	1	2	3	10	66	67	68
Sales	250	500	750	2,500	16,500	16,750	17,000
(-) Variable Cost	100	200	300	1,000	6,600	6,700	6,800
= Contribution	150	300	450	1,500	9,900	10,050	10,200
(-) Fixed Cost	10,000	10,000	10,000	10,000	10,000	10,000	10,000
= Profit / Loss	9,850	9,700	9,550	8,500	100	50	200

Why is Contribution called Contribution?

I now have a question for you.

**Take a closer look at the chart, and tell me, why is Contribution
called Contribution?**
In our example, the Contribution of one table is 150.
What is this a contribution towards?

Each table that Rita sells brings into her cash box a sum of 250. Then
shouldn't we be saying that the contribution of the table is 250?

You may, of course, point out that it would not be correct to call the
gross revenue as Contribution since to earn the 250 she has had to
incur expenses. Fair enough. Then let us deduct all the expenses (fixed
and variable) and call the resultant figure Contribution.

But it is neither the top line (Sales) nor the bottom line (Profit), but an
in-between figure that is called Contribution.

Can you tell me what this is a contribution towards?

> **Contribution is called Contribution because it is the contribution of each unit sold towards the organization's bottom line.**

Consider what the bottom line looked like when Rita was selling just one table.
There was a loss of 9,850.
She then made and sold the second table.
Her loss reduced to 9,700.
The Contribution of the second table towards reduction of the loss was 150.

At a sales level of 67 tables, the profit was 50.
When the 68th table was sold, the bottom line improved to 200.
What was the Contribution of the 68th table to the organization's bottom line?
Yes, it was 150 once again.

Contribution is called Contribution because it is the contribution of each unit sold TOWARDS the organization's BOTTOM LINE.

If an organization is making losses, with every increase in quantity sold, its losses will reduce to the extent of Contribution.
And if the business is already making profits, with every increase in sales, profits will increase to the extent of the Contribution of the quantity sold.

Bottom line is always impacted to the extent of Contribution.

Let's say that Rita's business has crossed the break-even point and is now selling 100 tables.

Let us draw out the profitability statement for a sales volume of 100 tables.

Per unit		100 tables
250	**Sales**	25,000
100	Variable Cost	10,000
100	Fixed Cost	10,000
200	**(-) Total Cost**	20,000
50	**= Profit**	5,000

On sale of 100 tables, the sales value, at the rate of 250 per unit, is 25,000.
The Variable Cost at 100 per unit works out to 10,000.
The Fixed Cost is also 10,000 and the effective Fixed Cost per unit would then be **100 (10,000/100)**.
The company, therefore, makes a profit of 50 per unit, or 5,000 for 100 units.

Now Rita calls a meeting of all the salespeople.
She tells them that she has some good news to share. They are all aware that theirs is a relatively new table-manufacturing organization and their break-even point is 67 tables. She is now very happy to inform them that, since the sales team has done a tremendous job, the organization has, in a short period of time, already broken even and today they have reached a sales volume of 100 tables, well above the break-even point!

She then shares the financial results with her team.
She informs them that today they are making a table at an in-house cost of 200 and selling it for 250.
Each table sold by the organization makes a profit of 50 and since they have sold 100 tables, at the rate of 50 per table, the organization's profit is 5,000.

> Bottom line is always impacted to the extent of Contribution.

Rita now exhorts them to carry on the good work that they are doing.
But she also warns them that there are competitors in the field, and it may happen that the competition may quote a price lower than theirs to get the business.

She informs her sales team that with this in mind, she is empowering them to be competitive and reduce the selling price of their tables, if required, as long as they don't accept orders at a loss.

Her instruction to the sales team is to sell the tables, as far as possible, at the stipulated selling price of 250.
However, if circumstances warrant, they may reduce the price at their discretion. But they must under no circumstances reduce the price to such an extent that the organization makes a loss.

Can Rita sell below cost and still make a profit?

Armed with these instructions, Neil, one of Rita's salespeople, quotes a price of 250 to a potential customer.

The competitor offers a similar table to the potential customer at 240.
Neil reduces his price to 230.
However, the competitor responds by lowering the price further to 215.
When Neil quotes 205, the competitor brings the price down to 200!

In this situation, what would you advise Neil to do?
Should he reduce his price even lower or let the competitor take the order?

Now let's assume that at this stage the potential buyer intervenes and says that their budget is only 150.
Neil has to decide whether he should accept the business at a price of 150 or reject it.

Rita has empowered the salespeople to reduce the price if need be, but under no circumstances to accept orders at a loss.

You will recall that in the early part of this book I defined financial management as *the ability on the part of every person in the organization to understand the impact of their actions on the organization's bottom line,* so that they make all those actions that strengthen the bottom line, and avoid those that hurt it.

Neil needs to be able to understand the impact of the decision to accept the order at a price of 150 on the organization's profit.
If it will increase the profits he should obviously say "yes".
If not, he must say, "no".

What was the profit that Rita's company was making when it was selling 100 tables?
If you look at the chart, you'll see that it was making a profit of 5,000.
This happened because the organization was selling tables for 250, which it made at a cost of 200.
It made a profit of 50 per table.
Having sold 100 tables at a profit of 50 each, the organization's profit was 5,000.

Now the 101st table is sold at 150.
We know that each table costs the organization 200.
On this table it appears to have made a loss of 50.

> A salesperson must never refuse a customer's offer out of ignorance or the inability to gauge the impact of the offer on the organization's profitability.

Since the profit on 100 tables is 5,000, and the loss on the 101st table is 50, therefore the profit on 101 tables should be 4,950 (that is 5,000 – 50).

Let us see if this is the correct answer.

Per unit		100 tables	101 tables
250	**Sales**	25,000	25,150
100	Variable Cost	10,000	10,100
100	Fixed Cost	10,000	10,000
200	(-) Total Cost	20,000	20,100
50	= Profit	5,000	5,050

The profit on selling 101 tables has increased to 5,050, and not fallen to 4,950.
Far from making a loss of 50, the organization has actually made a profit of 50.

A table that cost 200 has been sold at 150, and a profit has been made on the transaction!
How is this possible?

You can see how important it is to understand the concept of Contribution

Contribution is arrived at by deducting the Variable Cost from Sales, or the variable cost per unit from the selling price.
The 101st table is sold at 150 and its variable cost is 100.
This sale generates a positive Contribution of 50.
As I mentioned earlier, Contribution is so called as this is the Contribution of the unit sold towards the bottom line.

The profit on sale of 100 tables was 5,000.
The Contribution of the 101st table is 50.
Therefore profit on the sale of 101 tables is 5,050.

If salespeople in the field are to understand the impact of a decision to accept an order of additional units at a lower price on the organization's bottom line, they need to work out the Contribution of the item being sold.
Once they are confident that the Contribution is positive, they can go ahead with the sale.

Of course, there are many reasons why a salesperson may still say "no" to this offer even though the organization would not be losing money. This decision might have a negative effect on customers who have paid the full price. There may well be a comfortable market with many customers who are willing to pay the full price. But leaving these and other such reasons aside, a salesperson must never refuse a customer's offer out of ignorance or the inability to gauge the impact of the offer on the organization's profitability.

Perhaps you are thinking that the order can be accepted at a reduced selling price of 150 because Rita's organization has already broken even. On reaching the break-even point sales of 67 tables the organization has recovered the entire fixed cost of 10,000.

From the 68th table onwards there was no more fixed cost to be recovered. The only additional cost to be incurred for manufacturing an additional unit is the variable cost. And the excess of selling price over the variable cost (that is, Contribution) consequently becomes the additional profit.

> **This reasoning prompts me to ask whether such an offer could have been accepted had the organization not broken even.**

Let us assume that Rita is selling only 50 tables, well below the break-even point of 67.
The financials would look like this.

Per unit		50 tables
250	**Sales**	12,500
100	Variable Cost	5,000
200	Fixed Cost	10,000
300	**(-) Total Cost**	15,000
50	**= Profit / Loss**	2,500

Since the break-even point has not yet been reached, the organization is suffering losses.
The cost per table at this stage works out to 300.
Due to pressure from the competition, Rita is forced to sell at a price of 250.
With each table sold, the organization loses 50 and on selling 50 tables, it loses 2,500.

Clearly the company is struggling.

In this situation, Neil comes across a customer who shows great interest in buying a table from him, but has budgetary constraints and cannot afford a price beyond 150.
Neil now has to decide whether to accept this offer or not. Do you think he should do it?

> Financial Management is the ability on the part of every person in the organization to understand the impact of their actions on the organization's bottom line.

Let's see if conventional logic will give us an answer.

On a sale of 50 tables, the organization has suffered losses of 2,500.
This is because a table which is made at a cost of 300 is being sold at a price of 250.
50 tables are sold at a loss of 50 on each table.
The next table, if sold for 150, will entail a loss of 150 (selling price 150 less cost 300).
This means that the bottom line for 51 tables should reveal a loss of 2,650 (loss on 50 tables of 2,500 + loss on the 51st table of 150).

Let's see if this is correct.

Per unit		50 tables	51 tables
250	**Sales**	**12,500**	**12,650**
100	Variable Cost	5,000	5,100
200	Fixed Cost	10,000	10,000
300	**(-) Total Cost**	**15,000**	**15,100**
50	**= Profit / Loss**	**2,500**	**2,450**

Voila! The loss has not increased to 2,650 but rather has reduced by 50 and is now 2,450!
This also means that the organization has actually made a profit of 50 on this order!

Now how do we account for this?
When a table is sold at the rate of 250 the organization loses 50 per table – but when they sell it for 150 they earn 50!
How strange!

There is actually a simple reason.
I don't recall telling you at any stage that Contribution is called Contribution after reaching the break-even point!
Contribution is Contribution, period.

Even though Neil appears to have sold the 51st table at well below the average cost of 300 per table, this sale has still generated a positive contribution of 50 (150-100).

> I have pointed out earlier in this chapter that if the organization is making profits, for additional sales the profits will increase to the extent of Contribution. If it is suffering losses, losses will reduce to the extent of Contribution.

Can any sales or marketing person afford not to understand this?

Let's take a step back and view this with a larger perspective.

In the example we have discussed, imagine that the sales of the organization was 125 million, costs were 150 million, and the organization was losing 25 million.

There is a recession in the economy and a dearth of business. Every day the marketing chief or the CEO urges the sales team to go and find customers, failing which there is a possibility that the organization will go under, as it may not be able to sustain losses for much longer.

The sales team goes out desperately looking for business. A customer walks up to the salesperson. She is very keen to buy the tables, but can only afford the rate of 150 each.

What would be the typical reaction of this salesperson (invariably a so-called non-Finance executive!) to this offer?
This salesperson would probably refuse the offer, being under the impression that even when the tables are being sold at 250 each, the organization is on the verge of shutting down due to mounting losses.
The salesperson truly believes that if orders are accepted at 150, it would only serve to hasten the downfall.

But did anyone explore the possibility that perhaps it may have been easier to reach the revised break-even point by selling more numbers at the lower selling price than it was to reach an earlier break-even at a higher price?

You do realize that this person has committed a crime against the organization.

Had the salespeople accepted the order, where earlier the organization was losing 25 million, it would now be losing only 24.50 million.

Had they gone around looking for more customers who would be willing to buy at the reduced price of 150, perhaps this organization would survive where others were closing down.

One may, of course, point out that if they now start selling to every customer at the lower price, it will take that much longer to reach the break-even point.

But did anyone explore the possibility that perhaps it may have been easier to reach the revised break-even point by selling more numbers at the lower selling price than it was to reach an earlier break-even at a higher price?

This must also be a part of their strategizing.

Some practical examples showing application of marginal costing principles

Let us now take a few examples to understand the practical utilization of the knowledge of marginal costing to understand your business better, and for day-to-day decision-making purposes.

Example 1:

In this example we will see how marginal costing principles can be used to work out
- the break-even point,
- the profit at any level of sales and
- the sales to achieve any amount of profit for any organization,
by knowing just three numbers, namely, the selling price, the variable cost and the fixed cost.

Let's say we have the following information about three different businesses A, B and C as shown here.

	A	B	C
Selling Price per unit	200	200	200
Variable Cost per unit	50	80	100
Fixed Cost	30,000	30,000	30,000

Let's try and calculate in each case:
1) The break-even point
2) The profit on a sale of 400 units
3) The sales required to generate a profit of 90,000

1) To **calculate the break-even point**, we use the following **formula**:

$$\text{Break-Even Point} = \frac{\text{Fixed Cost}}{\text{Contribution per unit}}$$

We know the fixed cost. But we do need to work out the Contribution in each case. Contribution per unit can be calculated as Selling Price less Variable Cost. Applying the formula, we can calculate break-even point as shown here.

	A	B	C
Selling Price per unit	200	200	200
(-) Variable Cost per unit	50	80	100
= Contribution	**150**	**120**	**100**
Fixed Cost	30,000	30,000	30,000
$\dfrac{\text{Fixed Cost}}{\text{Contribution}}$	$\dfrac{30{,}000}{150}$	$\dfrac{30{,}000}{120}$	$\dfrac{30{,}000}{100}$
Break-Even Point	**200**	**250**	**300**

2) What will be the profit on a sale of 400 units?

Before we work out the profit let me tell you about the PV Ratio. Everyone involved in running a business must know its contribution margin as a percentage of sales. This, in marginal costing language, is called the PV Ratio or the Profit-Volume Ratio.

PV Ratio is calculated using the formula:

$$PV\ Ratio = \frac{Contribution}{Sales} \times 100$$

The PV Ratios work out to 75 percent in case A (150 / 200 x 100), 60 percent in case B (120 / 200 x 100) and 50 percent in case C (100 / 200 x 100).

What does PV Ratio indicate?
PV Ratio of 75 percent in the case of company A means that if A has sales of 100,000 it will generate a Contribution of 75,000 and if it generates sales of one million it will have a Contribution of 750,000.

Or
$$Contribution = Sales \times PV\ Ratio$$

> The only additional cost to be incurred for manufacturing an additional unit is the variable cost.

We need to find the profit on sale of 400 units in each of the above cases.

If A sells 400 units it will generate a sales value of 80,000. Since it has a PV Ratio of 75 percent, it will have a Contribution of 60,000 (80,000 x 0.75). From the Contribution if we now deduct the fixed cost of 30,000 we can see that the profit is 30,000. This means that if A sells 400 units it will earn a profit of 30,000.

In a similar way the profit in the case of B works out to 18,000 and in the case of C to 10,000 as shown in the table.

	A	B	C
Selling Price (400 units @200)	80,000	80,000	80,000
(x) PV Ratio	75%	60%	50%
Contribution	**60,000**	**48,000**	**40,000**
(-) Fixed Cost	30,000	30,000	30,000
Profit	**30,000**	**18,000**	**10,000**

Let's now convert this into a formula.
How did we arrive at the profit?
We multiplied the sales of 80,000 by the PV Ratio to arrive at the Contribution, from which we deducted the fixed cost.

Formula to find the profit at any level of sales:

$$Profit = (Sales \times PV\ Ratio) - Fixed\ Cost$$

3) What should be the sales to generate a profit of 90,000?

To arrive at the sales to generate a certain amount of profit we will have to work backwards.

The profit required is 90,000 and the fixed cost in each case is 30,000.

This means that in all three cases the Contribution required for a profit of 90,000 is 120,000.

$$Contribution = Fixed\ Cost + Profit$$

If Sales multiplied by PV Ratio gives us Contribution, then Contribution divided by PV Ratio will give us Sales.

Now if A needs a Contribution of 120,000 and the PV Ratio is 75 percent, then A will have to generate sales of 160,000 (i.e 120,000 / 75%)

$$Sales = \frac{Contribution}{PV\ Ratio}$$

In the case of B it works out to 200,000 (120,000 / 60%) and in the case of C to 240,000 (120,000 / 50%).

	A	B	C
Sales (Contribution/PVR)	160,000	200,000	240,000
Contribution	120,000	120,000	120,000
Fixed Cost	30,000	30,000	30,000
Profit	90,000	90,000	90,000

This table should be read from bottom to top

So what formula did we use to arrive at the sales?
We started with the desired Profit.
To this we added Fixed Costs which gave us the Contribution required.
We then divided the Contribution by the PV Ratio to arrive at Sales.

Formula to find the sales required to generate a certain amount of profit :

$$Sales = \frac{Desired\ Profit + Fixed\ Cost}{PV\ Ratio}$$

Example 2:

Sam makes exotic sandwiches which are loved and appreciated by everyone. He is often told by friends that he could make pots of money if he were to start a business supplying sandwiches to offices or for parties.

In order to make up his mind Sam wants to first know the break-even point of the business.

Let's say Sam decides to price a plate of sandwiches at 30.
The variable cost per plate (that is the cost of bread and other ingredients) works out to 10.
Sam would also have to incur a fixed cost per month (towards rent of the place to be used for business, staff salaries and so on) of 12,000.

The Selling Price per plate is	30
The Variable Cost per plate is	10
The **Contribution per plate** works out to	**20**
And the Fixed Cost is	12,000

Break-Even point can be calculated as

$$\text{Break-Even Point} = \frac{\text{Fixed Cost}}{\text{Contribution per plate}}$$

The break-even point, accordingly, works out to 600 plates per month (12,000/20).

If Sam feels that he can easily get far larger orders per month he will probably go ahead and set up the business.

To understand the profit that his business is making, Sam must now keep track of the number of plates of sandwiches sold per month.

If he sells say 1,000 plates in a month, Sam knows (without waiting for the accountants to compile the data and to prepare a Profit & Loss Account) that he has made a profit of 8,000.

Quantity (@ 30 per plate)	1,000 plates
Sales	30,000
(-) Variable Cost	10,000
= Contribution	20,000
(-) Fixed Cost	12,000
Profit	8,000

In the following month if he sells 2,000 plates, what would be the profit?

We do know that if Sam has made a profit of 8,000 on selling 1,000 plates, the profit will not double to 16,000 if sales double. Due to the leverage effect, which comes into play whenever there is an element of fixed cost in a costing structure, profits will increase more than proportionately.

Quantity (@ 30 per plate)	2,000 plates
Sales	60,000
(-) Variable Cost	20,000
= Contribution	40,000
(-) Fixed Cost	12,000
Profit	28,000

When the sales increased from 1,000 plates to 2,000 plates per month, the profit went up from 8,000 to 28,000.

When the Accounts Department submits the Profit & Loss Account to Sam showing a 250 percent growth in profit due to a 100 percent increase in sales, Sam will not be surprised.

In fact, he will be expecting it. With the help of marginal costing principles he had known this long before the accountants (who will arrive at the figure using a far more tedious method) could figure it out.

Sam now gets a bit ambitious and feels he must earn a minimum profit of 50,000 per month. He needs to know the sales that he must achieve to get the targeted profit.

Now he needs to calculate backwards. If he wishes to earn a profit of 50,000 and he has to bear fixed costs of 12,000, then his business must generate a Contribution of 62,000. And, in his case PV Ratio is 66.67 percent, that is, Contribution happens to be two-thirds of sales (on a plate of sandwiches which sells for 30, he makes a Contribution of 20).

> If an organization is making profits, for additional sales the profits will increase to the extent of Contribution. If it is suffering losses, losses will reduce to the extent of Contribution.

He must therefore generate a sale of 93,000 (3,100 plates at a selling price at 30 each). This can be arrived at by dividing Contribution by PV Ratio, that is 62,000/66.67%.

Quantity (@ 30 per plate)	3,100 plates
Sales	93,000
Contribution	62,000
Fixed Cost	12,000
Profit	50,000

This table should be read from bottom to top

Perhaps Sam feels that it would be difficult to increase the volume of sales at the existing price of 30 per plate, but he can definitely get more business if he were to reduce the price to 20 per plate.

Now he wants to find out the sales needed to achieve his desired profit of 50,000.

The new selling price is 20. The variable cost per plate will remain at 10. The Contribution will now drop to 10 and the relationship of Contribution to Sales (PV Ratio) is now 50 percent. This means that the Contribution is 50 percent of Sales, or in other words Sales is twice the Contribution.

To earn a profit of 50,000 Sam must generate a Contribution of 62,000 (50,000 + 12,000) for which he needs Sales of 124,000 (that is, twice the amount of contribution), or 6,200 plates at a selling price of 20 per plate.

Quantity (@ 20 per plate)	6,200 plates
Sales	124,000
Contribution	62,000
Fixed Cost	12,000
Profit	50,000

This table should be read from bottom to top

Before he takes a pricing decision, Sam must study the market and determine whether it will be easier to obtain orders for 3,100 plates of sandwiches at the old selling price of 30, or whether it would be easier to get orders for 6,200 plates at the reduced selling price of 20.

He must try and understand how price-sensitive the market is. Should he target up-market customers selling smaller volumes at bigger margins, or mid-market customers selling larger quantities at lower margins?

Only after this should he take a decision whether to sell his sandwiches on a food truck at a street corner, or through an outlet in an up-market mall; whether to serve sandwiches in paper plates or to use better quality crockery and cutlery; and the choice of newspapers to advertise in. These decisions make more financial sense if taken with an eye on the bottomline and not the other way round.

Example 3:

Should a business accept an order from a customer who is certain to go bad? Application of marginal costing principles will help in taking an intelligent decision.

The Hex Company usually offers its customers 30 days credit.

One customer offers to place a firm order of 10,000 pieces per month, if the credit period is extended to 60 days.

The company is aware this customer is asking for a longer credit because it is in a financial mess, and it is merely a matter of time that it becomes insolvent.

The per unit selling price and costs of the product are as follows:

Selling Price	30
Variable Cost	18
Fixed Cost	9
Profit	3

If the customer is expected to go bad after 6 months, should this order be accepted?

Let's work out the profitability of this order:

Sales	10,000 x 30	**300,000**
(-) Variable Cost	10,000 x 18	180,000
= **Contribution**	10,000 x 12	**120,000**
(-) Fixed Cost	10,000 x 9	90,000
Profit	10,000 x 3	**30,000**

Since the credit period is 60 days, an amount equal to two months' sales will always be in the pipeline.

Whenever this customer goes bad, the company stands to lose payment for two months of sales, which works out to 600,000.

If the customer becomes insolvent at the end of six months, assumably the company will have been paid for 4 months. The profit for four months works out to 120,000 (30,000 x 4).

If one does not apply marginal costing principles, the conclusion reached would be that since the loss (600,000) far exceeds the profit (120,000), this customer should not be entertained.

However, marginal costing gives us a different perspective.

This customer is a marginal customer, bringing additional business.

Will this company have to buy additional raw materials (incur additional variable cost) if this customer is accepted? Yes, of course.

Will this company have to pay additional rent (incur additional fixed cost) if this customer is accepted? No! Rent is being paid anyway.

For the marginal customer, fixed cost is irrelevant. And the contribution generated from the marginal customer is the profit.

How much will this company lose whenever this customer becomes insolvent? An amount equal to two months' variable cost, which is 360,000 (180,000 x 2).

And what would it have earned in the four months that it got paid for? 120,000 x 4 = 480,000. Application of marginal costing principles has brought about a paradigm shift in the thinking, and makes for more intelligent decision making. This can be critical when organisations are functioning well below capacity and during times of recession.

Example 4:

A business makes and sells two products A and B.
The details about selling prices and costs are as follows:

	A	B
Selling Price	50	100
Variable Cost	20	80
Contribution	30	20
PV Ratio	60%	20%
Fixed Cost	150,000	

The first thing the business must understand is its break-even point.
Now break-even point can be worked out using the formula:

$$\text{Break-Even Point (in units)} = \frac{\text{Fixed Cost}}{\text{Contribution per unit}}$$

This will give you the break-even point in units.
To calculate the break-even point in value use the formula:

$$\text{Break-Even Point (in value)} = \frac{\text{Fixed Cost}}{\text{PV Ratio}}$$

However this business sells two products with different PV Ratios and the break-even point will depend upon the sales mix of A and B.

Calculation of Break-Even Point under different combinations of sales mix

In case products A and B are sold in equal proportion then the weighted average PV Ratio works out to 40 percent and the business will break even on a sales of 375,000, as illustrated here.

Scenario 1

	PVR	Mix	PVR Weighted by Mix
Product A	60%	1	60%
Product B	20%	1	20%
			80%
Weighted Average PV Ratio =	$\dfrac{80\%}{2}$		= 40%
Break-Even Point =	$\dfrac{FC}{PVR}$ =	$\dfrac{150,000}{40\%}$	= 375,000

Since product A enjoys a far higher PV Ratio, the business decides to concentrate its energies more on selling product A.

In case the sales mix is now composed of 60 percent from product A and 40 percent from B (that is, in the ratio of 3:2), the average PV Ratio will improve to 44 percent and the break-even point can be achieved earlier on a sale of about 341,000.

Scenario 2

	PVR	Mix	PVR Weighted by Mix
Product A	60%	3	180%
Product B	20%	2	40%
			220%
Weighted Average PV Ratio =	$\dfrac{220\%}{5}$		= 44%
Break-Even Point =	$\dfrac{FC}{PVR}$ =	$\dfrac{150,000}{44\%}$	= 340,909

On the other hand, perhaps product B, while it has a lower PV Ratio, has a bigger market. In this case the mix may shift in favor of B (60 percent). The break-even point will now be reached at a higher sale of about 417,000. But it may be easier to achieve a sales level of 417,000 with three-fifths of sales coming from B than it would be to achieve a sale of 341,000 with 60 percent being contributed by A.

Scenario 3

	PVR	Mix	PVR Weighted by Mix
Product A	60%	2	120%
Product B	20%	3	60%
			180%
Weighted Average PV Ratio $=$		$\dfrac{180\%}{5}$	$= 36\%$
Break-Even Point $=$	$\dfrac{FC}{PVR} =$	$\dfrac{150{,}000}{36\%}$	$= 416{,}667$

Salespeople's performance and commissions paid to them

Now this organization decides to hire two salespeople, and to reward them by way of a 5 percent commission on sales.
Salesperson 1 sells 100 units of product A and 200 units of B, while Salesperson 2 sells 200 units of A and 100 units of B.

In our example A is sold for 50 per unit and has a PV Ratio of 60 percent and B is sold for 100 per unit and has a PV Ratio of 20 percent.

> It is extremely important to align the personal interests of the individual with the organization's interest so that both can benefit.

Now let's do a comparison of each salesperson's performance and the commission paid.

	Salesperson 1			Salesperson 2		
	Prod A	Prod B	Total	Prod A	Prod B	Total
Sales (units)	100	200	300	200	100	300
x Selling Price	x 50	x 100		x 50	x 100	
Sales (value)	5,000	20,000	25,000	10,000	10,000	20,000
x PV Ratio	x 60%	x 20%		x 60%	x 20%	
Contribution to Profit	3,000	4,000	7,000	6,000	2,000	8,000
Commission @5% of sales	250	1,000	1,250	500	500	1,000

Now look at what the business has, unwittingly, done.

Salesperson 1 has generated a Contribution of 7,000 for the organization and is rewarded with a commission of 1,250, whereas Salesperson 2 has earned 8,000 for the organization and been rewarded only 1,000!

An unintended conflict has been created between the organization's interest and the individual interest of the employee. *The individual earns more when the organization earns less and vice versa.*

It is extremely important to align the personal interests of the individual with the organization's interest so that both can benefit. This would have happened if the organization had fixed incentives based on Contribution and not on Sales.

This insight can only be obtained by applying the principles of marginal costing.

IMPORTANT EQUATIONS

Contribution

Three ways to arrive at Contribution:

$$\text{Contribution} = \text{Sales} - \text{Variable Cost}$$

$$\text{Contribution} = \text{Fixed Cost} + \text{Profit}$$

$$\text{Contribution} = \text{Sales} \times \text{PV Ratio}$$

Fixed Cost

$$\text{Fixed Cost} = (\text{Sales} \times \text{PV Ratio}) - \text{Profit}$$

$$\text{Fixed Cost} = \text{Contribution} - \text{Profit}$$

Profit-Volume Ratio

PV Ratio shows the relationship between Contribution and Sales. Generally it is expressed as a percentage. This ratio is **also known as Contribution-to-Sales ratio**. PV Ratio remains the same for any number of units provided Selling Price and Variable Cost are the same.

PV Ratio can be calculated in two ways:

$$\text{PV Ratio} = \frac{\text{Contribution}}{\text{Sales}} \times 100$$

$$\text{PV Ratio} = \frac{\text{Change in Profit}}{\text{Change in Sales}} \times 100$$

IMPORTANT EQUATIONS

Break-Even Point

BEP is the position at which there will be no profit and no loss. Sales in value will be equal to Total Cost and Contribution will be equal to Fixed Cost.

$$\text{Break-Even Point (in units)} = \frac{\text{Fixed Cost}}{\text{Contribution per unit}}$$

$$\text{Break-Even Point (in value)} = \frac{\text{Fixed Cost}}{\text{PV Ratio}}$$

Profit at a certain level of Sales

$$\text{Profit} = (\text{Sales} \times \text{PV Ratio}) - \text{Fixed Cost}$$

Sales required to earn a certain amount of Profit

$$\text{Sales (in units)} = \frac{\text{Fixed Cost} + \text{Profit}}{\text{Contribution per unit}}$$

$$\text{Sales (in value)} = \frac{\text{Fixed Cost} + \text{Profit}}{\text{PV Ratio}}$$

Profit is an opinion; cash in the bank is a fact.

Old Adage

CHAPTER

12

Leverage Analysis

How to calculate the Leverage Multiple,
its use in predicting profit, and
how to understand the risk profile
of any organization

In previous chapters I often used the term 'leverage'.

While discussing trading on equity we considered a situation where the sales were 100 and profits 20 in Year 1. In Year 2, we saw that if sales were to double to 200, the profit would rarely, if ever, just double. It would increase three or four fold or even more.

I called this disproportionate change in the bottom line brought about by a change in the top line the leverage effect.

At that point, I also pointed out that leverage is caused by the presence of fixed costs in the costing structure. This happens because when sales increase, the variable costs increase proportionately, but fixed costs do not increase. This results in a less-than-proportionate increase in the total cost – and a more-than-proportionate increase in the profit.

Here's another example:

	Year 1 100 units	Year 2 200 units
Sales	25,000	50,000
Variable Costs	10,000	20,000
Contribution	15,000	30,000
Fixed Costs	10,000	10,000
Profit	5,000	20,000

We can see that when sales increased from 25,000 to 50,000, profit increased from 5,000 to 20,000.
A 100 percent increase in sales resulted in a 300 percent increase in profit.

This is the leverage effect.

You will appreciate that if this organization had no fixed costs, then the Contribution and Profit would have been the same.

Now, if sales doubled, the profits (represented by Contribution) would merely double. There would be no leverage effect.

If sales were to double, the profit would rarely, if ever, just double.

On the other hand, if the fixed costs were even higher, the leverage effect would be even greater.

However if the fixed costs were higher, the organization's break-even point would also be achieved later since it would now have to produce and sell more in order to break even.

The term leverage is often used in the context of borrowing. An organization that borrows extensively is called a highly leveraged organization.

When an organization borrows, it has to bear higher interest costs. Interest is a fixed cost – and this is what leads to the leverage effect.

Interest, however, is not the only fixed cost that an organization bears. Other fixed costs would also have a similar effect.

The word **leverage** has been derived from the word **lever**, which is an engineering term.

Using a lever, it is possible to lift greater weights by exerting less effort. The lever works on the principle of fulcrum.

Similarly, when a highly-leveraged organization increases its turnover by a certain percentage, its profits increase by a larger percentage. The fulcrum in such cases is the fixed cost.

When fixed costs are higher, the impact on profit is greater.

Let's understand leverage

By now you are quite familiar with this equation of calculating profits:

Sales
(−) Variable Costs
Contribution
(−) Fixed Costs
Profit

Leverage is caused by the presence of fixed costs.

However, there are two types of fixed costs:
- **Operating fixed costs and**
- **Non-operating fixed costs**

Operating fixed costs are those that are necessary to run your operations. These include salaries, rents and overheads.

Non-operating fixed costs are those on which operations do not depend, in the sense that the operations would continue regardless of whether these fixed costs were incurred or not.
These are the financial fixed costs or interest.
Operations demand money. It does not matter to operations whether funds are procured from owners or from borrowed sources.
It's only when the money comes from lenders that there will be an interest cost.

> A disproportionate change in the bottom line brought about by a change in the top line is the leverage effect.

Since there are two types of fixed costs, the profit equation gets modified somewhat, as follows:

Sales
(–) Variable Costs
Contribution
(–) Operating Fixed Costs
Operating Profit or PBIT
(Profit Before Interest and Tax)
(–) Interest
(or Financial Fixed Costs)
PBT
(Profit Before Tax)

Of the two types of fixed costs, operating and financial, one is within your control and the other is not.

The fixed cost within your control is the financial cost. Whether to borrow or not to borrow is your choice. However, operating fixed costs are dictated by the nature of your operations. Are you a motor car manufacturer or a software development organization or a trader? Your operating fixed costs will, to a large extent, depend on your activity.

Two sides of the coin

The **advantage** of having high leverage is that when sales increase, profit increases at a disproportionate rate. Even a slight increase in sales will result in a substantial increase in profit.

However, there are two chief **disadvantages** of having high leverage:
Since, as pointed out earlier, leverage is caused by the presence of fixed costs (higher the fixed costs, higher the leverage), break-even point is achieved later.
Leverage works both ways. If profit increases at a disproportionately fast pace due to a certain increase in sales, profit will also decline at an equally fast pace if sales decrease.
As you can see, this is a double-edged tool.

What is a leverage multiple?

When sales increased from 25,000 to 50,000 in the example we saw earlier, and profit instead of merely doubling from 5,000 to 10,000, increased by three times to 20,000, who do you expect would be the most surprised of all?

In my experience, it's usually the people who are running the show themselves, the owners and the CEOs! So much so that at times they start doubting the accuracy of the accounts, and even question the accountant about how the profit has increased so dramatically.

> The term leverage is often used in the context of borrowing. An organization that borrows extensively is called a highly leveraged organization.

These owners and CEOs not only should not have been surprised, but they should have been expecting this very thing to happen.

How would they have known that if sales increased by 100 percent, profit would increase by 300 percent?

They would have known if they had been aware of the leverage multiple applicable in their case.

If the leverage multiple worked out to 3, they would know that a one-time impact on the top line would result in a three-time impact on the bottom line.

I will soon tell you how to calculate the leverage multiple.

Why is it important to know the leverage multiple?

Knowing the leverage multiple can help in two ways:
- It can help you predict profits. Since the multiple indicates the number of times the bottom line will be impacted, on account of a certain change in the top line, you can look at the change in sales compared to a previous period and estimate the profit.
- There will be times when you will feel the need to put an organization on a risk-scale. Calculating the leverage multiple can help you do this.

Maybe you meet a customer who can place a large order with your firm but demands an excessively long credit period. You don't want to say "no" and lose sizeable business. At the same time if you say "yes" and the client eventually cannot pay, you may end up losing substantial sums of money. If the offer comes from a low-risk customer, you may go ahead. If the customer falls into a high-risk category, you may want to decline. A look at the leverage multiple of the customer can help you make this decision.

Or perhaps you are a banker evaluating a proposal from a potential borrower. Calculating the leverage multiple and understanding the borrowers' risk profile will help you to decide whether to lend or not.

Similarly, as an entrepreneur, knowing the leverage multiple will guide you on your borrowing strategy.

How to calculate the leverage multiple

Since leverage is caused by the presence of fixed costs in the costing structure, and since, as we have now seen, there are two types of fixed costs, it follows that there are **two types of leverages** too. These are **Operating Leverages** and **Financial Leverages**.

Let us now see how to work out the multiplier factor for each of these.

Consider the following profit statement:

Sales	**100**
Less Variable Costs	20
= **Contribution**	**80**
Less Operating Fixed Costs (OFC)	60
= Profit Before Interest and Tax (PBIT)	20
Less Interest (FFC - Financial Fixed Cost)	16
= **Profit Profit Before Tax (PBT)**	4

As **Operating Leverage** is caused by the presence of Operating Fixed Costs, the formula to calculate the Operating Leverage Multiple is very simple. Just take the figure appearing before OFC and divide it by the figure after:

$$\text{Operating Leverage} = \frac{C}{PBIT} = \frac{80}{20} = 4$$

Similarly, **Financial Leverage** is caused by financial fixed costs and the formula is:

$$\text{Financial Leverage} = \frac{PBIT}{PBT} = \frac{20}{4} = 5$$

The **Combined Leverage** can be calculated as either Operating Leverage x Financial Leverage, which is 4 x 5 = 20, or as:

$$\text{Combined Leverage} = \frac{C}{PBT} = \frac{80}{4} = 20$$

What do these multiples indicate?

How does it help knowing that the Operating Leverage of this organization is 4, its Financial Leverage is 5, and its Combined Leverage is 20?

The Operating Leverage multiple tells us how a change in Sales will impact the PBIT.
The Financial Leverage indicates the impact of a change in PBIT on the PBT.
And the Combined Leverage shows the impact of a change in Sales on the PBT.

If we can call Sales the top line, PBIT the middle line, and PBT the bottom line, then:

- Operating Leverage shows the number of times the **middle line** will be affected due to a change in the **top line**.
- Financial Leverage indicates the number of times the **bottom line** will be affected due to a change in the **middle line**.
- The Combined Leverage shows the number of times the **bottom line** will be affected due to a change in the **top line**.

In this case, Operating Leverage is 4.
This means that if sales increase or decrease by 1 percent, the middle line will increase or decrease by 4 percent.

Here the Financial Leverage happens to be 5.
This tells us that if the middle line changes by 1 percent, the bottom line will change by 5 percent.

The Combined Leverage in this case is 20.
This means that if the top line changes by 1 percent, the bottom line will change by 20 percent.

Let us take the above profit statement again and see how we can use the leverage multiples to gauge profit.

> If the leverage multiple worked out to three, the management would know that a one-time impact on the top line would result in a three-time impact on the bottom line.

In our example, Sales is 100, PBIT is 20 and PBT is 4.
Now what will happen if Sales grow by 10 percent to 110?
As the Operating Leverage is 4 the PBIT will increase by 40 percent.
The existing PBIT is 20.
40 percent of 20 is 8.
Therefore the new PBIT will be 28.

The Financial Leverage is 5.
PBIT has increased by 40 percent.
Therefore the PBT will increase by 5 times of 40 percent, that is 200 percent.
Existing PBT is 4.
200 percent of 4 is 8.
The new PBT will accordingly be 12.

This can also be calculated by applying the Combined Leverage. The Combined Leverage is 20. Sales has increased by 10 percent. The PBT will therefore increase by 20 times of 10 percent, which is 200 percent. The existing profit of 4 will grow by 200 percent to 12.

Similarly PBIT and PBT can be calculated for any increase or decrease in Sales as shown here:

		Sales increase by 10%	Sales increase by 50%	Sales increase by 100%	Sales decrease by 10%
Sales	100	110	150	200	90
Less VC	20				
C	80				
Less OFC	60				
PBIT	20	28	60	100	12
Less Interest	16				
PBT	4	12	44	84	(4)

This can easily be verified by completing the table according to the conventional method of calculating profit:

		Sales increase by 10%	Sales increase by 50%	Sales increase by 100%	Sales decrease by 10%
Sales	100	110	150	200	90
Less VC	20	22	30	40	18
C	80	88	120	160	72
Less OFC	60	60	60	60	60
PBIT	20	28	60	100	12
Less Interest	16	16	16	16	16
PBT	4	12	44	84	(4)

Leverage Analysis
to gauge how risky an organization is

Let us now see how we can use Leverage Analysis to gauge how safe or risky an organization is.

Do you remember our discussion on Balance Sheets?
We saw that all Balance Sheets have to be one of just three possible types.

I would now like to tell you that if you take a Profit & Loss Account, re-classify the data as I've just explained, and calculate the operating and financial leverage multiples, you will discover that there are only **four types of organizations**.
The first type is one in which both Operating and Financial Leverages are high.
The second type would be one in which both Operating and Financial Leverages are low.
Type three may have a high Operating Leverage and a low Financial Leverage.
And **the fourth type** would have a low Operating Leverage but a high Financial Leverage.

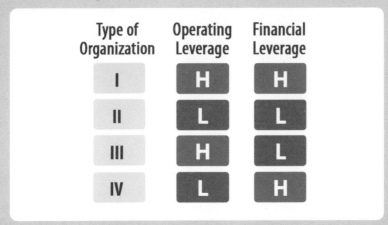

Type of Organization	Operating Leverage	Financial Leverage
I	H	H
II	L	L
III	H	L
IV	L	H

A relevant question at this stage would be, "How does one define High and Low leverage?"

These are relative terms and it may be difficult to put a precise number to what constitutes high.

I can, however, tell you what would be considered low.
A leverage of 1 is low.
A leverage of 1 would mean that if the turnover increases by 100 percent, profit would also increase by 100 percent.
Or, a 10 percent increase in sales would result in a 10 percent increase in profit.
No leverage benefit at all.

> As a lender, calculating the leverage multiple and understanding the borrowers' risk profile will help you to decide whether to lend or not.

In my opinion a leverage of 3 is high.
Consider the case of a business where the operating and financial leverage multiples are 3 in each case.
This means that the combined leverage is 9.
This would mean that a 10 percent increase in sales will result in a 90 percent increase in profit.
Wonderful!

However, a reduction of only 10 percent in turnover would bring about a 90 percent drop in profit. Almost the entire profit could get wiped out with a relatively small drop in sales. This could cripple the organization.

Let us now understand how to read and interpret leverages to analyze the health of an organization.

Rating the Type I organization

The first type of organization we are considering has a **high Operating Leverage**.

Type of Organization	Operating Leverage	Financial Leverage
I	H	H

Now when is Operating Leverage high?
Yes – only when the Operating Fixed Costs are high.

As we saw a short while ago, Operating Fixed Costs are, by and large,
beyond the control of the organization. They are dependent on the
nature of its activities.
The Type I organization thus seems to be one that, by virtue of the
nature of its business, must bear high Operating Fixed Costs.
This gives us an inkling that the break-even point of this organization
will also be achieved relatively late since it has to generate sufficient
Contribution to recover a higher Operating Fixed Cost.
Once the organization breaks even, it will begin to enjoy the benefit of
leverage by default.
Every small change in turnover, post break-even, will lead to
substantial increase in profits.

**We have gauged all this information just by looking at the letter
H under the column Operating Leverage.**

Let's now look at its **Financial Leverage**, which is **also high**.
A high Financial Leverage would indicate that the interest burden
is high.
This gives us a peek into the temperament of the management as
regards borrowing.
They seem to believe in liberally supplementing their own resources
with borrowed capital.

This would push the company's break-even point even further.
It would now have to work harder, and make and sell more, in order to
recover the additional burden of interest cost.

But the combined leverage is so high, that once the organization
breaks even (which would be achieved at a substantially high level of
installed capacity), the slightest change in sales would take the profit
zooming up. Of course, the scope for this is limited, since this
organization may soon reach the limit of its installed capacity.

However, even a small depression in sales will bring profit sliding
down, and the organization may even start making a loss.

How would you rate this organization on a risk scale of one to 10 (one being low-risk and 10 being high)?

I would put it in a range of 8 to 10.

If this organization approaches you with an offer of a large order, but demands a 6-month credit period, how comfortable would you be to take it on as a customer?
Not comfortable at all!

> As an entrepreneur, knowing the leverage multiple will guide you on your borrowing strategy.

When it approaches a bank for a loan, you will agree that the bank is going to be reluctant to entertain its proposal.

However, as long as it is making profit, it may be worth investing in its shares as a short-term proposition – while recognizing that it is a somewhat risky investment. If its sales continue to rise, there is scope for phenomenal gain.
Having invested, you would need to watch it carefully, and exit at the first sign of a downward trend.

Rating the Type II organization

The second type of organization has a **low Operating Leverage**.

Type of Organization	Operating Leverage	Financial Leverage
II	L	L

This means that its Operating Fixed Costs are on the lower side.
This appears to be a lucky organization since the fixed costs that it must bear, and over which it has no control, are less.
This also means that on operations it has a quick break-even.
The company is very likely to break even on a relatively lower level of its installed capacity.

It has a long way to go before it reaches full capacity utilization.

We now turn our attention to the **Financial Leverage**, and find that this is **also low**.
This tells us that the organization has a low burden of interest.
It appears to be conservative in its approach towards borrowing.
Even though it achieves break-even relatively quickly, it does not believe in hastening its pace of growth with the help of borrowed resources.
Therefore, it appears to be an organization which probably has a slow and sluggish, but continuous, growth.

If this kind of organization approaches you with an offer of a large order provided you extend it a long credit period, go right ahead. However, it's very unlikely that this organization will come to you with such a request because it clearly does not believe in borrowing.

If this organization goes to a bank for a loan (which in all likelihood it will not) the bank would be very happy to entertain its proposal.

If such an organization is issuing shares, stay away. You will probably make more money keeping your investment as a fixed deposit on interest with this organization than from investing in its stock.

Rating the Type III organization

In this case the **Operating Leverage is high**.

Type of Organization	Operating Leverage	Financial Leverage
III	H	L

Which means its operating fixed costs are high.
The organization has no control over these.
The fixed costs that it is forced to bear are on the higher side and the break-even point would be achieved at relatively higher levels of capacity utilization.

The benefit of leverage would automatically accrue after the break-even point is reached, where a small increase in sales would lead to a disproportionately greater increase in profits.

However the **Financial Leverage is low,** and this means that the borrowings are kept under check.

How would we describe the management's temperament? Conservative?
I would not call it conservative. A more appropriate word is "sensible".
This organization recognizes that it already has a high Operating Leverage.
If it borrows, its Financial Leverage will also become high and it will then become like the Type I organization.
Leverage analysis has guided this organization not to borrow.

> Leverage is a double-edged tool. If profit increases at a disproportionately fast pace due to a certain increase in sales, profit will also decline at an equally fast pace if sales decrease.

Or, perhaps, it did attempt to borrow but the banker examined its leverage and refused to lend.
It has offset the risk of high Operating Leverage by keeping its Financial Leverage under control.

Rating the Type IV organization

In this case the **Operating Leverage is low.**

Type of Organization	Operating Leverage	Financial Leverage
IV	L	H

This tells us that its Operating Fixed Costs are low.
This in turn means that the fixed costs over which there is no control are low.

The break-even point on operations is quick.
This organization will probably break even on a lower capacity utilization.

And the **Financial Leverage is high**.
It would appear that this organization, recognizing its fortunate situation whereby it breaks even relatively quickly on operations and has a long way to go before it reaches full-capacity utilization, decided to accelerate its pace of growth with a generous dose of borrowed capital.

However, it has still not become a very risky proposition since the risk that borrowing entails has been largely offset by the safety of its operating leverage which is on the lower side.

This is therefore the best combination to have.

The Type I organization is excessively risky. It should not have borrowed, but it has.
The Type II organization is safe but conservative. It could have borrowed to its advantage, but does not.
The Type III organization should not and does not borrow. Leverage analysis guided it to keep a check on its borrowings.
Such organizations must fund expansions from their own resources or through a public issue of shares.
The Type IV organization can afford to borrow and it does.
Such organizations quicken their pace of growth without becoming unduly risky.

Money is like a sixth sense – and you can't make use of the other five without it.

Somerset Maugham
(1874 - 1965)
English Playwright, Novelist and Short-story Writer

CHAPTER
13

Funds-Flow Analysis

How to read a Funds-Flow Statement

Learn to read the numbers,
trace the sources and uses of funds
of your organization, talk to figures
and make them talk back to you

What is a funds-flow statement?

A funds-flow statement is a statement that traces the sources and uses of funds of an organization.

Every organization must prepare a funds-flow statement.

You might wonder why, when an organization is already making a Balance Sheet in which the liabilities represent its sources of funds and the assets its uses, it should duplicate its efforts and prepare another statement that provides the same information.

While a Balance Sheet lists sources and uses, it is not a perfect substitute for a funds-flow statement. It has certain limitations.

Take a look at the Balance Sheet given below:

Balance Sheet

Liabilities		Assets	
Share Capital	300	Fixed Assets	750
Reserves	200		
Long-Term Loans	400	Current Assets	300
Current Liabilities	150		
	1,050		**1,050**

Do you see any flaw in this Balance Sheet from the point of view of flow of funds?

A Balance Sheet does reveal sources and uses.
It does tell you WHERE the money has come from and WHERE it has gone and the amount of funds that have been received and applied.

However, what it fails to reveal is WHEN the money came in and WHEN it went out.

Remember, a Balance Sheet only represents the situation at one particular point of time.

Suppose the Balance Sheet shown here is as on 31 December of a particular year.

> A Balance Sheet does tell you WHERE the money has come from and WHERE it has gone... what it fails to reveal is WHEN the money came in and WHEN it went out.

The Balance Sheet informs you that as on 31 December the owners' contribution to this business was 300.

But when did the owners contribute this money?

It could have been last week. Or it could be that the owners started this business 25 years ago, invested 300 as their capital and, till date, haven't taken it back. Where is the flow?

A Balance Sheet is a static document.

On the other hand, a Funds-Flow Statement spans a period of time.

We need to know how much money has come in and how much has gone out over the last one year, the amount of funds flowing in and out over the last one month and so on.

If the Balance Sheet does not reveal funds flow, then from where can we get the information to prepare a funds-flow statement?

The data will still come from the Balance Sheet.

But for this, we will need not one but two Balance Sheets.

If we wish to make an annual funds-flow statement, we will need this year's Balance Sheet as well as the previous year's Balance Sheet.

If we wish to make a weekly funds-flow statement we will need two Balance Sheets one week apart.

How is a Funds-Flow Statement made?

Even though this chapter is not about how to make funds-flow statements but how to read them, let me give you a quick, over-simplified version of how these statements are made.

Consider the two Balance Sheets shown (revealing the previous year's and the current year's figures).

Balance Sheet

Previous Year	Liabilities	Current Year	Previous Year	Assets	Current Year
100	Share Capital	300	600	Fixed Assets	750
75	Reserves	200			
500	Long-Term Loans	400	175	Current Assets	300
100	Current Liabilities	150			
775		**1,050**	**775**		**1,050**

Look at each figure on the Liabilities' and the Assets' sides and try to reach a conclusion whether there has been an inflow of funds or an outflow.

The first item on the Liabilities' side is Share Capital.
Up to the previous year it was 100 and this year it has increased to 300. Share Capital can only increase when fresh shares have been issued, which brings an inflow.
This organization appears to have issued shares to the tune of 200 during the last one year.
So we show this on the Sources' side of the Funds-Flow Statement.

The next item is Reserves & Surplus which have also increased by 125 over these two years.
Since profits retained in the business get transferred to Reserves, this will also be shown as a Source.

Long-Term Loans have decreased by 100. This can be on account of repayment, which would be shown as a Use.

Fixed Assets have increased. It appears that assets have been purchased and therefore 150 would also appear on the Uses' side.
Now, we still have to take into account the changes in Current Assets

and Current Liabilities. Since **Current Assets less Current Liabilities** represent Net Working Capital (NWC), we will take into account the change in NWC. Therefore a typical Funds-Flow Statement will usually be accompanied by another Statement Showing Changes in Working Capital.

Statement showing Change in Working Capital

	Previous Year	Current Year
Current Assets	175	300
(-) Current Liabilities	100	150
= Net Working Capital	**75**	**150**
Increase in Working Capital	**75**	

The net working capital has increased by 75. This means that the organization has invested more money in working capital, and this amount will therefore be shown as a Use.

Funds-Flow Statement

Sources		**Uses**	
Shares issued	200	Loans repaid	100
Retained profits	125	Fixed assets purchased	150
		Increase in Working Capital	**75**
	325		**325**

This Funds-Flow Statement reveals that, while the Balance Sheets may have shown 775 and 1050 as Sources and Uses in the two years respectively, the funds flowing in and out during that period are to the tune of 325.

The Sources' side reveals that of the 325, the organization has earned only 125. The balance has been raised through an issue of shares.

However, the question uppermost in the minds of most businesspeople is, "But where is the money?"
If 325 has come in, why is the bank account not richer by this amount? Where has the money gone?

The answer to this question can be obtained by looking at the Uses' side of the Funds-Flow Statement.

The Uses' side informs the reader that 100 was used to repay loans, another 150 was used to purchase fixed assets, and an additional 75 was pumped into working capital.

> Businesses earn. But the question uppermost in the minds of most businesspeople is, "But where is the money?"

It thus becomes possible for an organization to trace all the money that has come in and gone out.

The managers are now also in a position to check whether long-term funds are being used for long-term purposes and short-term funds for short-term purposes – or not.

What I have illustrated through this example is actually an over-simplified version of how funds-flow statements are made.
The actual preparation of these statements is far more complicated and intricate.

How is a Cash-Flow Statement different from a Funds-Flow Statement?

A cash-flow statement is prepared from transactions affecting cash only. A broader approach is adopted to interpret the term funds taking into account all financial resources.

Cash flow is determined on the basis of three components by which cash enters and leaves a business:
1) Core operations,
2) Investing activities and
3) Financing activities

Cash flow statements are useful to identify the current liquidity problems.

A funds-flow statement analyses the sources and applications of funds of long-term nature and the changes in working capital. It tallies funds generated from various sources with various uses to which they are put and determines the financial consequences of business operations.

A funds-flow statement is useful to find answers to questions such as:
- If profits are increasing year after year, why is our liquidity deteriorating?
- How were the proceeds of the equity issue utilized?
- How was the new plant funded?

A funds-flow statement is based on an accrual accounting system and is very useful for long-range financial planning.

How to read a Funds-Flow Statement

All the key people of an organization must learn and refine their skills of financial management. The ability to read and understand a Funds-Flow Statement is an important component of these.

Take a close look at the Funds-Flow Statement shown here and see what insights you can get about the organization to which it pertains.

Funds-Flow Statement

Sources		Uses	
Profit	400,000	Redemption of bonds @ 5% premium	210,000
Decrease in Working Capital	**700,000**	Plant purchased	900,000
Sale proceeds of investments	250,000	Dividends paid	240,000
	1 350,000		**1 350,000**

Statement showing Change in Working Capital

	Year 1	Year 2
Current Assets		
Inventories	1 200,000	800,000
Debtors	500,000	560,000
Bank Balance	240,000	80,000
(A)	1 940,000	1 440,000
Current Liabilities		
Short-Term Loan	--	50,000
Creditors	1 000,000	1 150,000
(B)	1 000,000	1 200,000
Net Working Capital (A) – (B)	**940,000**	**240,000**
Decrease in Working Capital	**700,000**	

Note: Sales of the company has remained constant over the two years.

Look at each figure carefully, try and talk to it. Make the numbers come to life by getting into them and seeing what exactly they mean and represent. Don't proceed until you have spent time reading and understanding this Funds-Flow Statement.

Do you estimate that this business is healthy or not?
Is it headed towards prosperity or trouble?
Given the opportunity, would you like to invest in the shares of this company?

Now let's see what we can read from the Funds-Flow Statement.

In this example there are a number of aspects on which we will not be able to comment since our data is insufficient. For instance we do not know what kind of business is being run, what the product is, or how much the turnover is.

Let us see what we can conclude with the limited information available.
All I want you to keep in mind is that if this had been a real-life case, we would have had access to far more information and we would have gained far greater insight than what we will now.

A cursory glance at the statement shows that of the 1.35 million in-flow, 400,000 has come from profits.
It is not possible to comment on the quantum of profits since, while the footnote says that sales over the two years have been constant, it is silent as to whether the profit is also constant or greater or less than the previous year.
If, with constant sales, the profit is lower than the previous year, it is a negative sign; if the profit is higher than before, it is positive.
However, this appears to be a profit-making organization and that is a good sign.

The working capital has been reduced drastically.
Despite this, sales have been constant.
Being able to maintain the top line with substantially lower working capital at its disposal also appears to be a sign of efficiency.

The company has disposed of some investments and generated an inflow of 250,000.

Investments appearing in a Balance Sheet usually indicate an investment made outside one's own business. Healthy organizations, those that are constantly growing and expanding, will usually want to re-invest all available funds in their own businesses.

Investments, unless they are strategic, or in one's own subsidiary or sister-concern, or those made with the intention of taking over the company in which investments are being made, could be indicative of stagnation in the existing businesses.

This organization appears to have invested money outside its business in earlier years, but during the current year it has felt the need to dispose of the investments and plough the money back into its own business.

To that extent, this also appears to be a positive sign.

The uses reveal 210,000 being used towards redemption of bonds, which is at a premium of 5 percent.

This organization must have issued bonds and borrowed 200,000 at some time in the past.

In the absence of information, it will be logical to assume that the bonds must have matured during the year under consideration.

The organization, therefore, seems to have honoured its commitment of repayment of loans to the bond-holders and, as a token of its appreciation, has returned the loan with a premium of 5 percent for good measure.

Honouring commitments, and repayment of debts, that too at a premium, gives this company a few more brownie points.

A plant has been purchased at a cost of 900,000, which forms a major part of the uses of funds.

Buying a plant, which results in the creation of more capacity, is indicative of the organization planning expansion and growth, which is definitely a positive sign.

And finally the organization has also distributed dividends of 240,000 amongst its shareholders.

The amount distributed, in absolute terms, does not reveal anything about the percentage of dividend since we don't know the amount of share capital.

However, we do know that the profit earned by the organization is 400,000 and dividends distributed are 240,000 which amounts to 60 percent of the profit.

What is distributed is called 'pay-out' and the portion of profits that get transferred to Reserves is called 'pay-in'.

A 60:40 pay-out : pay-in ratio is generous by any standards.

If you were contemplating investing in this company, this could be one of its most attractive features.

Everything about this company seems to be fine. It is a profit-making company, efficient (as reflected by the ability to maintain its top line despite reduced working capital), is selling its investments and ploughing back the money into the business, repaying its debts on time, expanding its capacity for production and growth, and generously rewarding its shareholders.

Someone who does not know how to read financial statements, or someone who has not read this book, would probably conclude that this organization is in terrific shape.

What is the real picture?

While analyzing this Funds Flow Statement, did we apply a single rule that I have explained earlier in this book? Did we calculate any ratio? What we have done just now is an emotional analysis of the statement.

Let's take another look at this Funds-Flow Statement, check the application of the rules of good financial management, and re-assess our comments on the health of this business.

The first area of concern in this statement is the footnote, which says that the sales over the last two years have been constant.

I would usually not recommend investing in an organization unless the sales graph is facing skywards. There are thousands of companies to choose from. Why would anyone want to go out of their way and invest in a company whose sales have either started stagnating or falling? This footnote worries me.

However, let me not be hasty and write this company off merely on the basis of a footnote.

I have always felt that the function of a Funds-Flow Statement is less to supply answers and more to help you frame the right questions, about which you should seek information. One can then form opinions based on the information so received.

So before I reach any conclusion I would like to meet an important functionary of this organization, preferably the CEO, and ask a couple of questions.

Q1. Why have your sales stopped growing?
Q2. Even though your sales have not increased, why have you made this substantial investment in a plant?

What if the CEO smiles pleasantly and tells me that their sales not growing is nothing to worry about.
The sales have remained the same not because they did not have orders – they are in fact overloaded with orders – but because they ran out of capacity.
It's precisely for this reason that they have made an investment in a new plant.

An answer like this would obviously bring about a paradigm shift in my outlook. My concern about sales not increasing, as also about the investment in plant, have been alleviated.

But now I have another question for the CEO.

If the organization has plenty of orders on hand, and now the capacity has also been created, it would mean that the company expects to produce and sell more in the coming months.

> A funds-flow statement analyses the sources and applications of funds of long-term nature and the changes in working capital.

It is also natural, therefore, that to support the increased levels of activity, the company will need larger amounts of working capital.

However, the Funds-Flow Statement is showing a drastic reduction in working capital.

So my next question to the CEO is: How do you explain this contradiction? On one hand, you have purchased a plant, indicating increased levels of activity. On the other, we can see that a large portion of the money required to fund the purchase has come through a reduction of working capital!

I now begin to fear that even if this organization is flush with orders, and also has the requisite installed capacity to increase production, I very much doubt if it will be able to do so. It seems to me very likely that it is going to run short of working capital.

Keeping this doubt at the back of our minds, let us first do a clinical analysis of this Funds-Flow Statement and see if the company has complied with the fundamental rules of Good Financial Management which demand that healthy organizations:

- must use long-term funds for long-term purposes;
- must use short-term funds for short-term purposes;
- MAY use long-term funds for short-term purposes; but
- must NEVER use short-term funds for long-term purposes.

Let's evaluate how the organization fares on this front.

Funds-Flow Statement

Sources		Uses	
Profit	400,000 LTS	Redemption of bonds @ 5% premium	210,000 LTU
Decrease in Working Capital	700,000 STS	Plant purchased	900,000 LTU
Sale proceeds of investments	250,000 LTS	Dividends paid	240,000 LTU
	1 350,000		1 350,000

The profit of 400,000 is a long-term source.
So is the sale proceeds of investments of 250,000.
However 700,000 from reduction of working capital is a short-term source.
This means that the total long-term sources amount to 650,000 and the short-term sources to 700,000.

On the Uses' side, redemption of bonds of 210,000 is a long-term use.
Purchase of a plant, 900,000, is also a long-term use.
So is the dividend distribution of 240,000.

Or, since dividend is necessarily a distribution of profits, a better way of looking at this would be to eliminate 240,000 from the Uses' side as well as from the profits on the Sources' side.
The new equation that emerges is:

> **Total long-term sources = 410,000**
> (profits after deducting dividends
> + sale proceeds of investments)
> **Short-term sources = 700,000**
> (reduction of working capital)

However, **the entire utilization of funds of 1110,000 is on the long-term account!**

> **The function of a Funds-Flow Statement is less to supply answers and more to help you frame the right questions.**

It is obvious that this organization has been guilty of using short-term funds for long-term purposes!

This, as you know, is absolutely not done.

The question that now arises is: Can we condone them for this crime? The crime of using short-term funds for long-term purposes?

Perhaps we cannot quite condone it, but the severity of the crime may reduce if we find that this organization had at its disposal so much excess working capital that, despite reducing 700,000, the working capital that it is left with continues to be adequate not only for its current needs, but also for the increased requirements which are going to arise when the new plant begins to operate.

Reducing working capital, by itself, is not a crime.
In fact, any organization that has an excess investment in working capital (or, for that matter, in any asset), must reduce and bring it to an optimum level.

So, let us now take a look at the **statement showing change in working capital** again and see if this organization can afford to reduce its working capital.

Statement showing Change in Working Capital

	Year 1	Year 2
Current Assets		
Inventories	1 200,000	800,000
Debtors	500,000	560,000
Bank Balance	240,000	80,000
(A)	1 940,000	1 440,000
Current Liabilities		
Short-Term Loan	--	50,000
Creditors	1 000,000	1 150,000
(B)	1 000,000	1 200,000
Net Working Capital (A) – (B)	940,000	240,000
Decrease in Working Capital	700,000	

A healthy organization will ensure that it maintains a Current Ratio (current assets: current liabilities) in the region of 2:1 and a Quick Ratio (liquid assets: current liabilities) of a minimum 1:1.

The Current Ratio in year 1 works out to 1.94 : 1
(1940,000 / 1000,000), which is close to the norm of 2 : 1.
In year 2, it has reduced drastically to 1.2 : 1
(1440,000 / 1200,000) which is way below the norm.

As I have explained earlier, Current Ratio falling below the norm may not, by itself, be a cause for concern as long as the Quick Ratio is maintained at 1:1 or more.

So let's now quickly calculate the Quick Ratio.
The Quick Ratio in year 1 is 0.74 : 1
(740,000 / 1000,000), well below optimum.
In year 2, it has fallen further to 0.53 : 1
(640,000 / 1200,000), which is even lower.

This organization had a good Current Ratio in year 1, which has become bad in year 2.
It had a bad Quick Ratio in year 1 itself, which has become worse in year 2.

Does this appear to be an organization which can afford to reduce working capital?
Certainly not!

Now let's go into the details of the working-capital statement to understand how the reduction in working capital has been effected.

The company has reduced its inventory from its previous levels of 1200,000 to 800,000.

Now at first glance, this may appear to be a sign of efficiency. It may be argued that this organization has managed to maintain its turnover despite a 33 percent reduction in its inventory levels, and this reflects efficient inventory management.

I might normally have agreed with this point of view, but in this case I do not.

In this particular case, had the inventory of 1.2 million remained at 1.2 million, I would have called it a reduction of inventory in real terms. This is because in the current year the company has made a huge investment in plant, indicating that it plans to produce and sell more. This means it would need even more inventory. For the inventory level to have remained constant in this situation is actually an effective reduction of inventory.
What I simply cannot understand is that on the one hand, the organization is planning increased production, and on the other, the physical inventory is actually going down!
This definitely does not reflect efficiency, but rather shoddy inventory management, giving rise to a fear that even though the company now has improved capacity and will be looking at increased levels of production, it is probably going to run out of inventory and will not be able to achieve production targets.

The next item in the working capital statement is debtors. These have risen from 500,000 to 560,000.

Now, the amount due from debtors increasing is fine, as long as sales also increase.

However, the footnote has told us that sales are constant. Debtors have no business to increase in the absence of an increase in sales!

With constant sales, debtors can go up only in two ways.

Either the old customers are delaying payments, or the organization is being forced to offer longer periods of credit to achieve the same sales value. Both of these are negative signs.

The next item shows that the bank balance has fallen from 240,000 to 80,000.

Money lying in the bank is the most obvious of all non-performing assets.

At the same time, a less-than-necessary bank balance would mean an inability to meet expenses and commitments on time.

Therefore bank balance, like the investment in all other assets, should be at an optimum level.

We are also aware that organizations must maintain a minimum liquidity ratio of 1:1.

When this organization had a bank balance of 240,000 it had a liquidity ratio lower than 1, indicating a need for increased liquid assets. A further reduction in bank balance to one-third of its erstwhile level indicates an alarming deterioration of the situation, as reflected by the worsened Liquid Ratio of 0.53:1.

The next item reveals that the organization has taken a fresh short-term loan of 50,000.

This should have actually increased the bank balance. And despite this the bank balance has reduced.

The reduction in bank balance is even more than it appeared at first to be!

As we can see, creditors have increased from 1 million to 1.15 million.

Just as in the case of debtors, if the organization has purchased more and thus owes more to creditors, it's fine. But in this case, sales are constant. Therefore production and consumption of materials must also be constant and creditors should be constant too.

I'm afraid not.

I agree that sales, production and consumption of raw material must be constant. But where do you get the material to consume from? You must either purchase material to consume it, or you must consume material already available in the warehouse.

Part of this organization's requirement of material has been met from the stocks held (indicated by the reduced inventory levels).

Now if consumption is constant, and if part of the requirement is met from existing inventory, this means that the current year's purchases must have been lower than before.

If the purchases were lower than before, the company should also owe creditors less than before.

So how do we now explain this contradiction: the company has purchased less but it owes its creditors more?

This can only mean that the old creditors are not being paid.

This is the only way in which an organization can have reduced purchases and still owe more.

What can we conclude from all this?

This organization appears to be in serious trouble. Its sales are not increasing. Its collections are inefficient. Its liquidity is so poor that it seems unable to pay its vendors on time.

In this situation a few questions to the management might be in order.

And the first question is – why was the plant purchased?

Nothing in this example seems to justify the purchase of a plant. But let's give them the benefit of the doubt. Perhaps the organization did indeed need the plant, for reasons which are not apparent to a reader of the funds-flow statement.

If they were so keen to purchase the plant they should also have realized that this was a long-term use of funds, and they should have organized a long-term source to finance it.

But apparently they were so desperate to acquire the plant that when they could not organize long-term resources, they deemed it fit to release money from working capital and divert it for a long-term use, not understanding that this investment would actually result in a further additional requirement of working capital and they would soon be trapped in a vicious cycle.

The next question must pertain to the wisdom of redeeming bonds.

This organization's liquidity is already in such bad shape, due to its inability to increase sales or to make timely collection from its debtors, that it is unable to even pay its creditors on time.

Yet, it seems to be paying off its bond holders.

Now the management may point out that this amount was due to be paid, since the bonds had matured.

However, the amount to the creditors was also due and should have been paid.

Ideally, organizations must make timely payment to all whom they owe. And if it is not possible to pay everybody,
an order of priority has to be followed.

You must have noticed, throughout the book, whenever I showed you a Balance Sheet, the items on the Liabilities' side always appeared in the same order.

Balance Sheet

Liabilities	Assets
Share Capital	Fixed Assets
Reserves	
Long-Term Loans	Current Assets
Creditors (Current Liabilities)	

There is a reason for this.
This also represents the order of payment, which is from the bottom up.

If you don't have sufficient money to pay everybody and can pay only one, then pay your creditors, the vendors or suppliers. They are your lifeline. If you don't pay them and they stop the supply of materials, your entire functioning can come to a standstill.

Having paid creditors, if you have money left, you now pay other long-term lenders. And after paying all outsiders, the last to be paid will be the owners.

Now here is an organization that is not paying creditors – but it has gone and repaid the bond-holders, and that too at a premium!

Why should any company pay a premium?

Premium is a sign of excessively good health.

This organization is floundering.

The bond redemption could have been delayed and the premium should certainly not have been paid.

But what really takes the cake is that the management has the audacity to distribute 60 percent of the profits among owners as dividends, even though the creditors are daily being denied their due payment!

> When you can hold a conversation with numbers, when you can talk to figures and make them talk back to you, when financial statements begin to lose their mystery, it is then and only then that you can begin to romance numbers.

All said and done, this organization is in dire straits. Unless the management takes immediate steps on a war footing to set things right, it may not be long before the entire organization goes under.

Through this funds-flow statement, I wanted to illustrate how, when you know how to read numbers, they can come to life.

When you can hold a conversation with numbers, when you can talk to figures and make them talk back to you, when financial statements begin to lose their mystery, it is then and only then that you can begin to romance numbers.

If you want to feel rich,
just count the things
you have that
money can't buy.

Proverb Quotes

CHAPTER

14

Creating Financially Intelligent Organizations

It is not enough for only a handful of individuals within an organization to possess commercial acumen

Having gone through the book so far, I'm quite sure you will agree with me that it is not enough for only a handful of individuals within any organization to possess commercial acumen.

Good Finance Management is the cumulative result of smart financial decision-making on the part of every individual.

For many years now, I have been engaged in helping *individuals* become financially intelligent.

We, at Lamcon, are now working toward creating **Financially Intelligent *Organisations*™ (FiOs)**

How does this work?

The process of creating **FiO**s includes:

- Studying the organization structure and the role of each employee
- Providing relevant training in finance to *everybody* in the organization, at all levels
- Carrying out a diagnostic study of the accounting system / ERP software in place and suggesting changes, if required
- Determining the various MIS reports to be generated and recommending who should be the recipients of different reports.
- Training the recipients to read, interpret and take actions based on the information contained in those reports
- Hand-holding and providing consultation for a certain period of time to help bring about improvements
- And then certifying the organization to be Financially Intelligent

An integral part of **FiO** is providing training to *everybody* in the organization, from top to bottom.

This will be done through:

- Live face-to-face training programs of varying durations, depending on the employees' level and role, ranging from one-half day to three days or more.

- Permitting access to online training programs

- Creating a library of videos which can be viewed from time to time to refresh the concepts learnt

- Providing books and material to each employee to be used as ready reference

It is my hope and dream that, in the years to come, bankers and lenders will be willing to lend and potential shareholders will agree to invest only if the organization is certified as a Financially Intelligent Organisation.

Do write to me if the concept appeals to you and you wish to get your business certified as an **FiO** at **anil@lamconschool.com**

The cost of a thing is
the amount of what I call
life which is required
to be exchanged for it,
immediately or
in the long run.

Henry David Thoreau
(1817-1862)
American Author, Poet and Philosopher

CHAPTER
15

Financial Literacy For All

In order to have a more meaningful impact, it is important that everybody is financially literate

All this while I have been talking of finance management as the prerogative of the wealthy.

For more than twenty years, Lamcon has provided financial education to corporate houses at the senior most levels of management, within India and internationally.

Over the years, I have had the pleasure of seeing the participants of my programs benefit from what they have learned. They have found financial relief, growth and success and have used their learning to address the root causes of the different problems their businesses have faced.

However, all my efforts have been directed towards those who are relatively well-off.

While this has been very successful, **I have also come to realize that in order to have a more meaningful impact, it is important that India, as a nation, should become more financially literate.** All people, across all social boundaries, should know how their actions affect their work-places financially. They should also have the ability to handle their own finances better. In fact, every individual and every family must learn to manage their finances well for their sustained well-being and growth.

It is a commonly-held view that citizens of prosperous nations are prosperous. However, it is my firm belief that when the individuals of a nation learn to manage their finances efficiently, that nation is bound to be prosperous.

There are large segments of our population which could benefit greatly from the kind of learning that we, at Lamcon, provide but will never have the opportunity to attend such a program.
These include small traders, employees at the lowest rung of the corporate ladder and the under-privileged members of society who work hard all day long to scrape together a living. Sometimes they find the cost of obtaining such education prohibitive.
Invariably, though, they just do not have the awareness of how important these skills are.

There are small businesspeople for whom it is just as important to understand the principles of good financial management as it is for the largest corporate house.

There are traders who, for want of an understanding about the proper use of money and cash flow, drive their businesses deeper into loss, even when they could have been very profitable.

There are housewives of low income and lower-middle-class homes whose families could benefit greatly if they understood a few basic facts about savings and investments.

As a socially conscious Indian I have often felt that I have a responsibility towards the less privileged sections of society.

I am also keenly aware that for India to continue its phenomenal growth, it is important that each and every individual in this country should be financially literate.

With this in mind I began to make efforts to impart financial literacy among the underprivileged sections of society.

Over a period of time, these adhoc programs organized by Lamcon have culminated in a very ambitious project which we have named **Financial Literacy For All: a movement towards creating a financially intelligent India.**

Embarking on this long journey, we first divided the target audience into six subgroups, and created course outline and material for each one. These subgroups are:

1. **Non-managerial cadre employees and workers within corporations:** This is a segment to which employers usually do not provide financial training and do not invest in. But when workers at the lowest rung also understand how their actions bring profits for the organization – and in turn to themselves – they also get a sense of achievement and this surely leads to higher productivity and improved bottom lines.

2. **Small business owners/traders and professionals:**
   This category needs to understand good finance management practices as much as a large organization does, but usually does not spend time and money to acquire these skills.

3. **School children:** The subject of finance is so important that this understanding should be inculcated in the minds of children at an early age.

4. **Non Governmental Organizations (NGOs):** If NGOs also understand financial management they can probably benefit a larger number of beneficiaries with their limited resources.

5. **Housewives:** When housewives understand financial management better, they will handle their home finances better.

6. **Underprivileged and lower-income group citizens such as domestic staff, day-wage earners and contract employees, hand-cart vendors and others:** This is the most exploited section of all. Many vegetable vendors borrow as little as Rs 90 each morning, use this money to buy vegetables from the wholesale market, hawk their wares all day long, and in the evening they return Rs 100 to the money lender. What they don't realize is that they are paying interest at an effective annual rate of over 4000 per cent. To get out of this trap, if they can manage to save Rs 5 each day for just about 18 days *(or for that matter, Re 1 for 90 days)*, they can create their own cycle of Rs 90. Somebody has to reach out and explain this to them.

The target audience is One Billion Indians.

I naturally cannot do it alone. But I have created a train-the-trainer program and am in the process of recruiting groups of volunteers to join me in my mission. If each of these volunteers trains more volunteers (besides one of the target segments to which they have access), we will soon have an army of trainers which can help India sustain its growth momentum and become more prosperous.

As a reader of this book, and now in full possession of the principles of financial management, I would consider you to be an ideal candidate to participate in Lamcon's efforts.

You could do this by:
- enrolling as a volunteer trainer
- using Corporate Social Responsibility programs of your company to spread our message
- enlisting the media to help us in our goals.

If you would like to participate, please email me at **anil@lamconschool.com**.

I look forward to hearing from you!

Anil Lamba

Live & Online Training Sessions on Finance Management

Program Details

1 Global Business Managers
One Day Program on Finance Management

2 Finance Fundamentals
One Day In House Training Program on Finance for Non Finance Persons

3 Personal Tax Planning
One Day Program on Personal Tax Planning

4 Eye on the Bottom Line
Two Day In House Training Program on Finance for Non Finance Managers

5 Costing and Budgeting
Two Day In House Training Program for Costing and Budgeting

6 Financial Acumen for Sustainable Growth
Three Day In House Training Program for Finance for Non Finance Persons

7 Cash is King
Three Day Program on Finance Management

8 Finance for Business Leaders
Four Day Program on Finance Management

9 Building Business Acumen
Five Day In House Training Program for Finance for Non Finance Persons

10 Understanding Numbers™
Two Day Program on Finance for Non Finance Persons (Public Program)

11 Finance Edge™
Nine Week Intensive Program on Finance Management (Public Program)

Call : +91.99 22 351 352
Email : training@lamconschool.com
Website : www.lamconschool.com

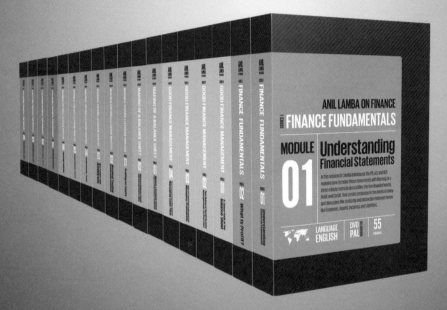

ORDER FORM

ANIL LAMBA ON FINANCE | A series of Training Films on Finance Managment

SERIES I
FINANCE FUNDAMENTALS

The two modules in this series are intended to lay a strong foundation for understanding the financial principles discussed in subsequent sessions. Using easy-to-understand, jargon-free language, Dr Lamba introduces the two most important financial statements, and eliminates a number of misconceptions usually associated with commonly-used-yet-often-misinterpreted terms.

		Price	Qty	Amount
MODULE **01**	**Understanding Financial Statements** Duration: 55 mins Format: DVD PAL	₹2850 US $ 64.50		
MODULE **02**	**What is Profit?** Duration: 60 mins Format: DVD PAL	₹2850 US $ 64.50		

SERIES II
GOOD FINANCE MANAGEMENT

Financial mismanagement is responsible for most business failures the world over. Even the global economic meltdown towards the end of the first decade of this millennium is primarily attributed to financially disastrous decisions.
In this series, Dr Lamba gives his mantra of Good Finance Management and expounds on his Two Golden Rules. Organizations that abide by these rules achieve sustained growth and success and those that violate can suffer serious consequences.

		Price	Qty	Amount
MODULE **01**	**A closer look at the Balance Sheet** Duration: 38 mins Format: DVD PAL	₹2850 US $ 64.50		
MODULE **02**	**Two Rules of Good Finance Management:** An Overview Duration: 27 mins Format: DVD PAL	₹2850 US $ 64.50		
MODULE **03**	**Rule 1 of Good Finance Management:** Managing Profitability Duration: 47 mins Format: DVD PAL	₹2850 US $ 64.50		
MODULE **04**	**Rule 2 of Good Finance Management:** Managing Cash Flow Duration: 69 mins Format: DVD PAL	₹2850 US $ 64.50		

SERIES III
MAKING OF A BALANCE SHEET

The usual perception is that it takes years to learn how to make Profit and Loss Accounts and Balance Sheets. Dr Lamba teaches, in a very quick and simple way, how to make these financial statements in, both, the accountants' as well as laypersons' way.

		Price	Qty	Amount
MODULE 01	**Making a Balance Sheet – without any knowledge of accounting** Duration: 44 mins Format: DVD PAL	₹2850 US $ 64.50		
MODULE 02	**Making a Balance Sheet – the accountants' way** Duration: 38 mins Format: DVD PAL	₹2850 US $ 64.50		

SERIES IV
MARGINAL COSTING AND LEVERAGE ANALYSIS

Application of Marginal Costing principles is essential to take financially profitable decisions. In the six modules comprising this series, Dr Lamba explains complicated marginal costing concepts in such an easy and interesting way that will make you wish you had known about it arlier.

		Price	Qty	Amount
MODULE 01	**Trading on Equity** Duration: 47 mins Format: DVD PAL	₹2850 US $ 64.50		
MODULE 02	**Marginal Costing – Break-Even Analysis** Duration: 46 mins Format: DVD PAL	₹2850 US $ 64.50		
MODULE 03	**Cost-Volume-Profit Analysis** Duration: 34 mins Format: DVD PAL	₹2850 US $ 64.50		
MODULE 04	**Marginal Costing – Cases I** Duration: 51 mins Format: DVD PAL	₹2850 US $ 64.50		
MODULE 05	**Marginal Costing – Cases II** Duration: 57 mins Format: DVD PAL	₹2850 US $ 64.50		
MODULE 06	**Leverage Analysis** Duration: 44 mins Format: DVD PAL	₹2850 US $ 64.50		

SERIES V
EVALUATING FINANCIAL PERFORMANCE

In this series two very important tools of evaluating financial statements, Ratio Analysis and Funds Flow Analysis, are explained.

		Price	Qty	Amount
MODULE 01	**Ratio Analysis** Duration : 42 mins Format: DVD PAL	₹2850 US $ 64.50		
MODULE 02	**Ratio Analysis – Cases** Duration : 49 mins Format: DVD PAL	₹2850 US $ 64.50		
MODULE 03	**Funds Flow Analysis – How to read Funds Flow Statements** Duration : 53 mins Format: DVD PAL	₹2850 US $ 64.50		
MODULE 04	**Funds Flow Analysis – How to make Funds Flow Statements** Duration : 43 mins Format: DVD PAL	₹2850 US $ 64.50		

Please note : Shipping & handling charges will be extra

Enclosed is Cheque/Demand Draft No. _____ dated _____
drawn on _____ bank for
rupees _____
in favour of Lamcon Finance & Management Services Pvt Ltd.

Name : _____
Designation : _____
Company's Name : _____
Address : _____
_____ Pin : _____
Phone No : _____
E-mail : _____
Signature : _____

SCAN THE QR CODE

OR DOWNLOAD THIS
ORDER FORM ONLINE
www.lamconschool.com/
downloads/alf-
orderform-2013.pdf

BANKING DETAILS
ACCOUNT NAME : LAMCON FINANCE & MANAGEMENT SERVICES PVT LTD
ACCOUNT NUMBER : 01482560000665
NAME OF BANK : HDFC Bank Ltd
BRANCH : East Street Branch
ADDRESS : 2418 East Street, Pune 411001, India.
RTGS/NEFT IFSC : HDFC0000148
SWIFT Code : HDFCINBB